WASHINGTON, D.C.
Wonder and Light

PHOTOGRAPHY BY
JEAN-LOUIS MONFRAIX

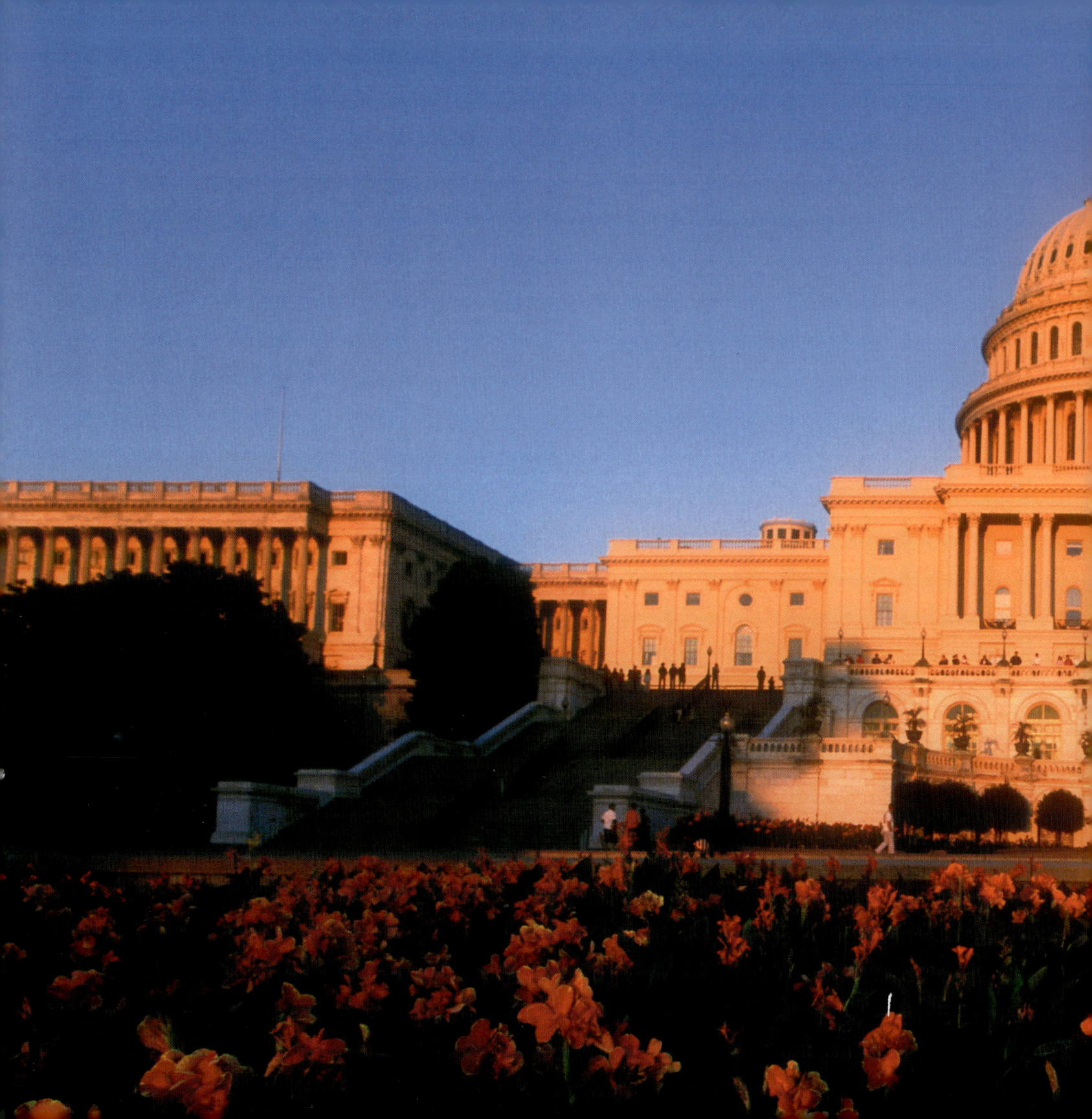

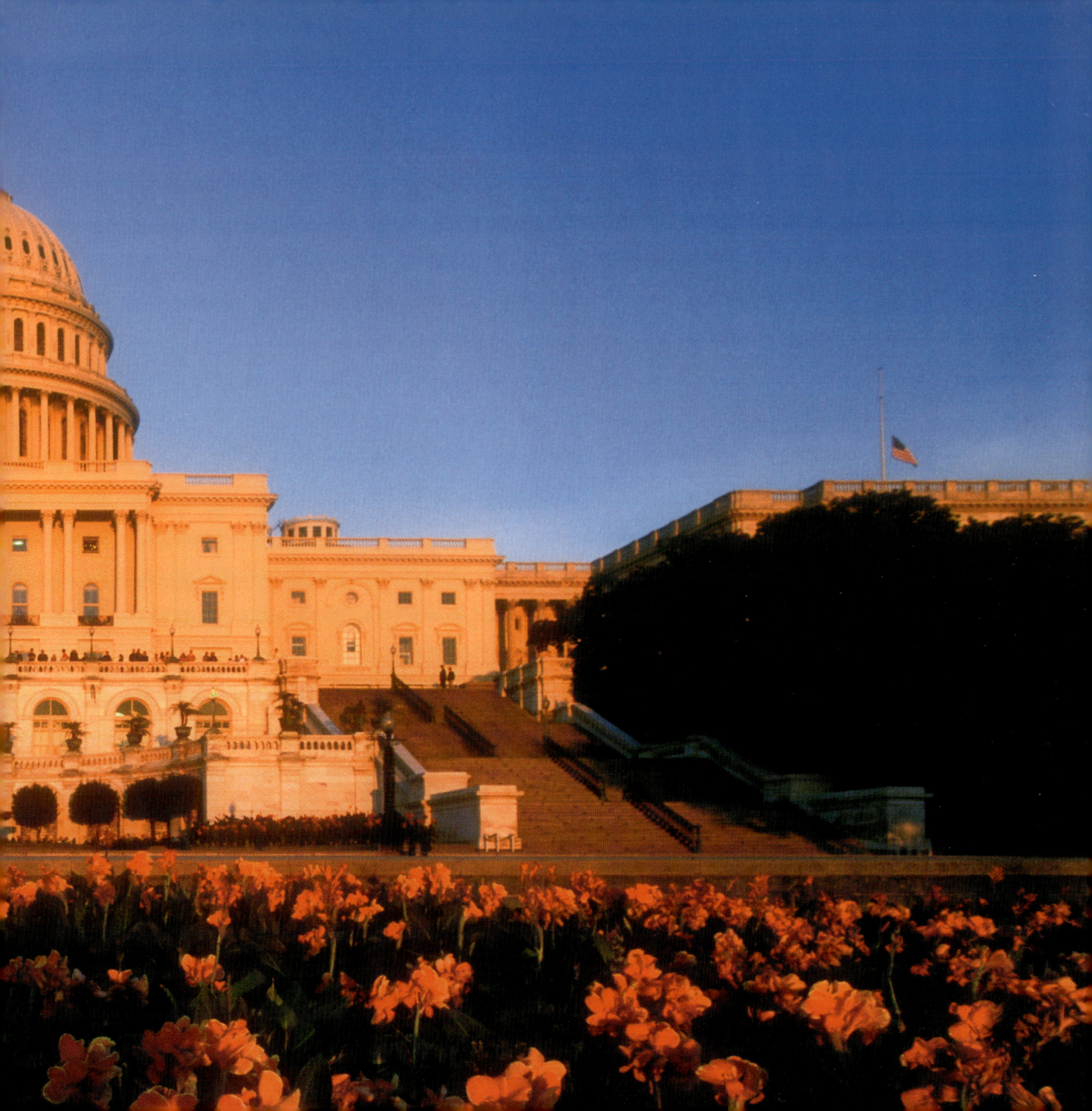

WASHINGTON, D.C.
Wonder and Light

Photography by
Jean-Louis Monfraix

Mountain Trail
——————— Press

1818 Presswood Road • Johnson City, Tennessee 37604
www.mountaintrailpress.com

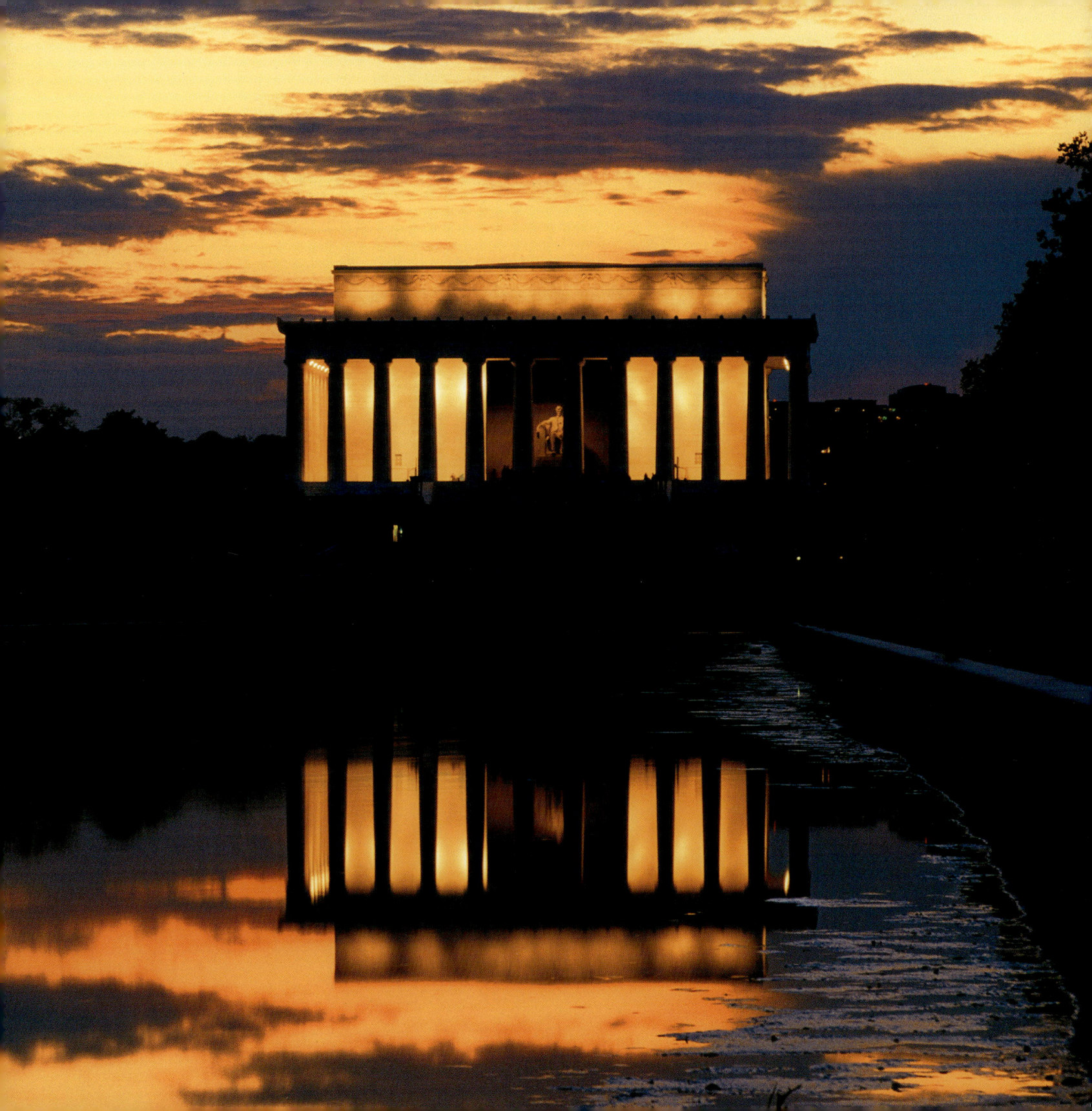

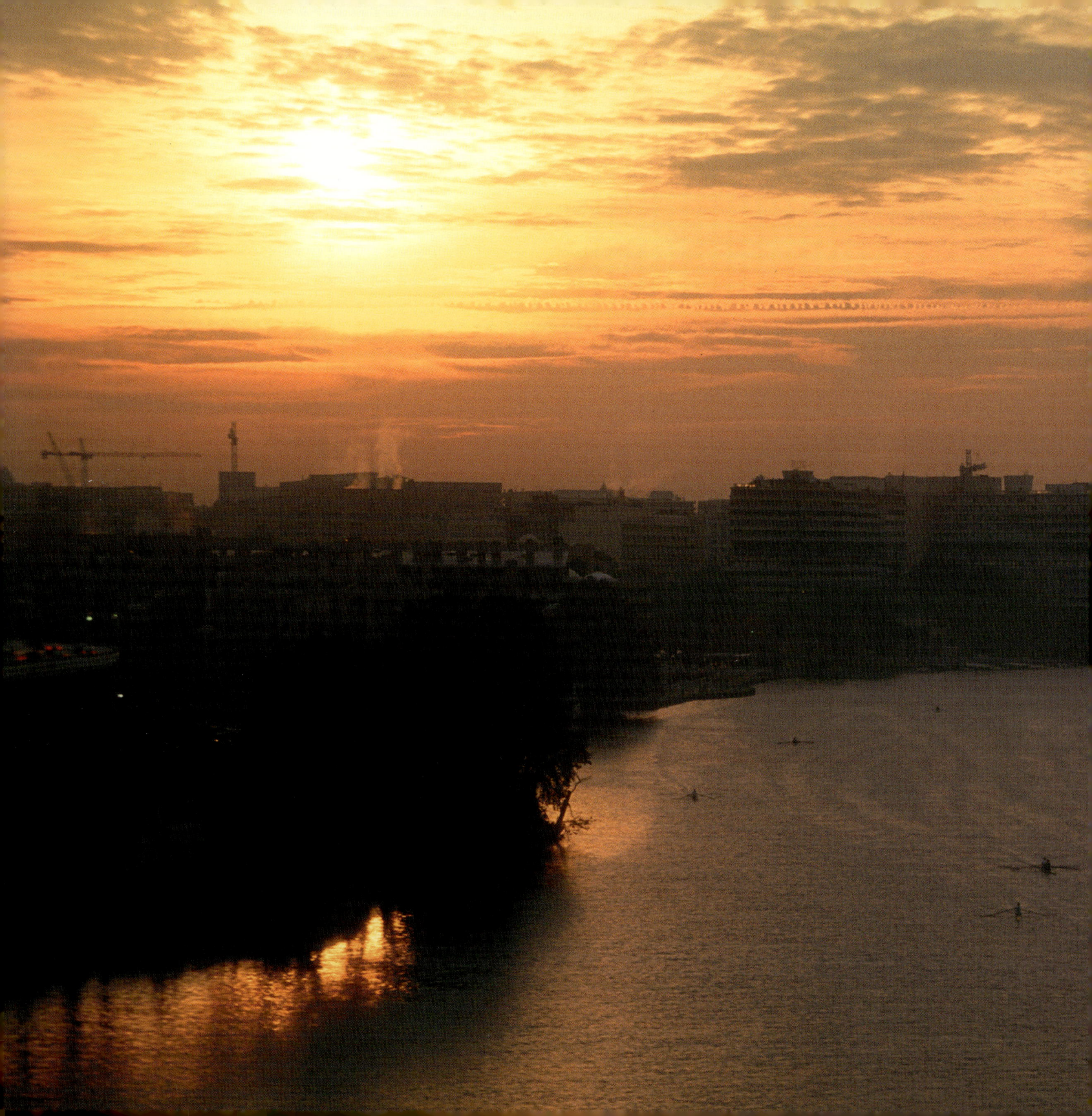

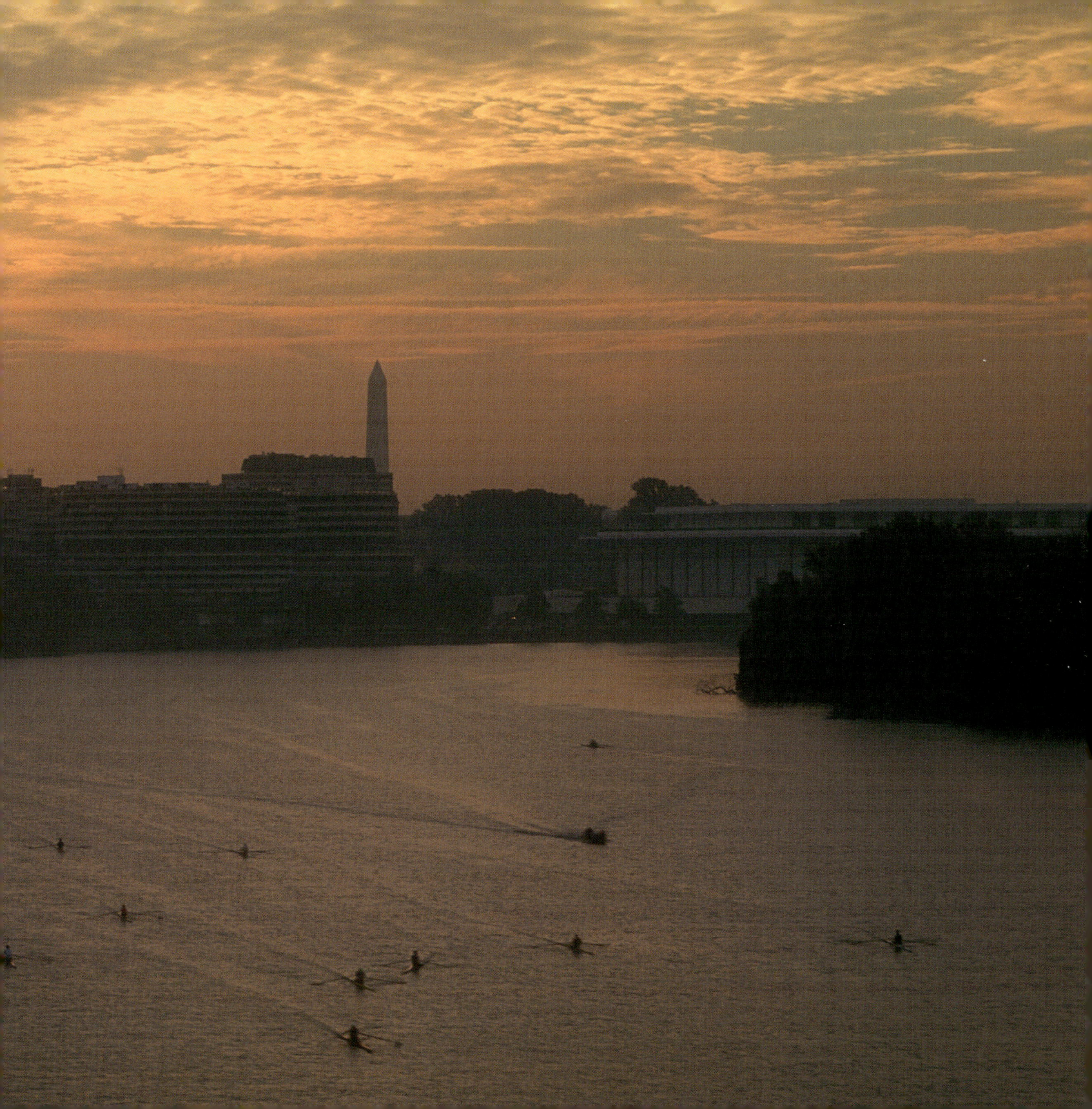

WASHINGTON, D.C.
Wonder and Light

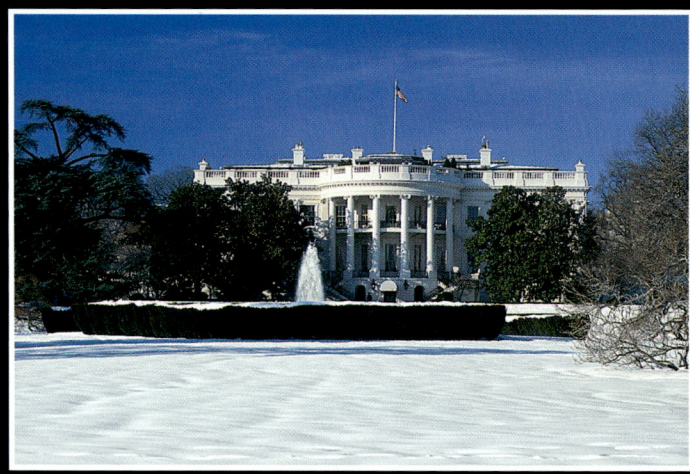

Jean-Louis Monfraix

Book design: Ian J. Plant
Entire Contents Copyright © 2006 Mountain Trail Press LLC
Photographs © Jean-Louis Monfraix
All Rights Reserved
No part of this book may be reproduced in any form without written permission from the publisher.
Published by Mountain Trail Press LLC.
1818 Presswood Road
Johnson City, TN 37604
ISBN: 0-9770808-2-X
Printed in Korea
First Printing, Spring 2006

Front cover: Independence Day fireworks over the National Mall's most prominent landmarks: the Lincoln Memorial, the Washington Monument, and the Capitol Building.
Title page: Another burst of fireworks over the National Mall.
Full page spread: The Capitol, taken just three days after the September 11th terrorist attacks. Washingtonians can be seen gathering on the terrace as they prepare to observe a candlelight vigil.
Second title page: The Lincoln Memorial mirrored in the Reflecting Pool at sunset.
Preceding pages: Sunrise over the Potomac River.
Right: Fresh snow on the grounds of the Capitol.
Above: The White House in winter.

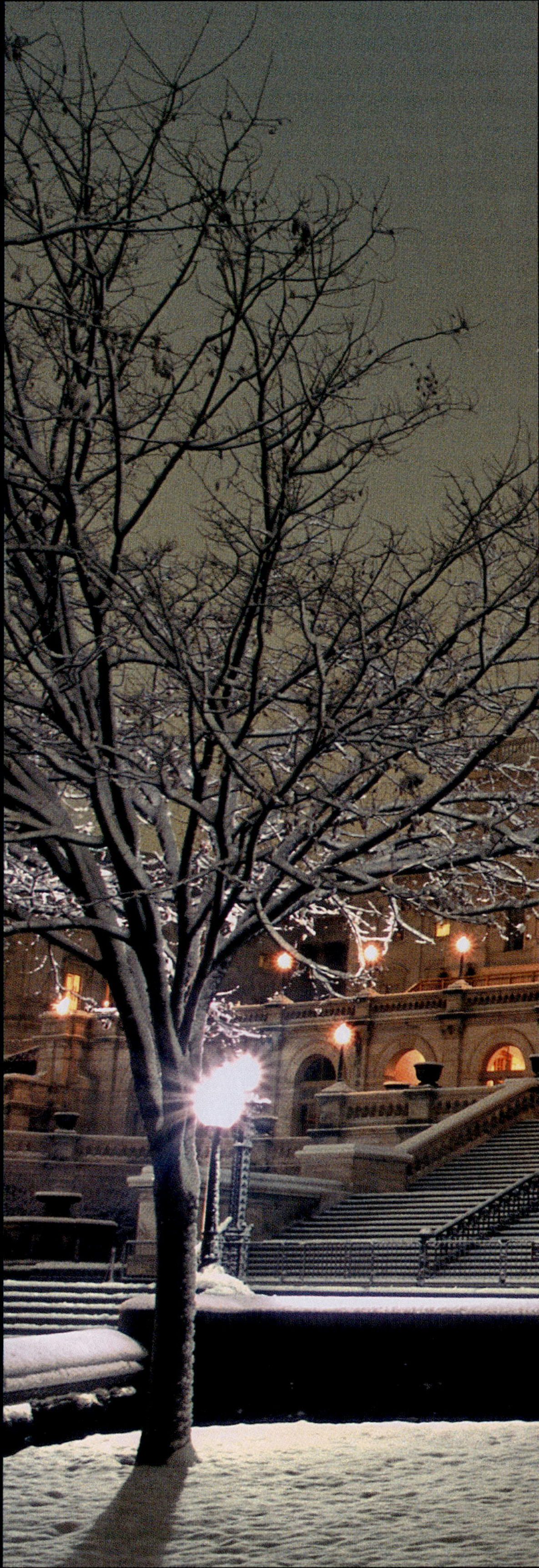

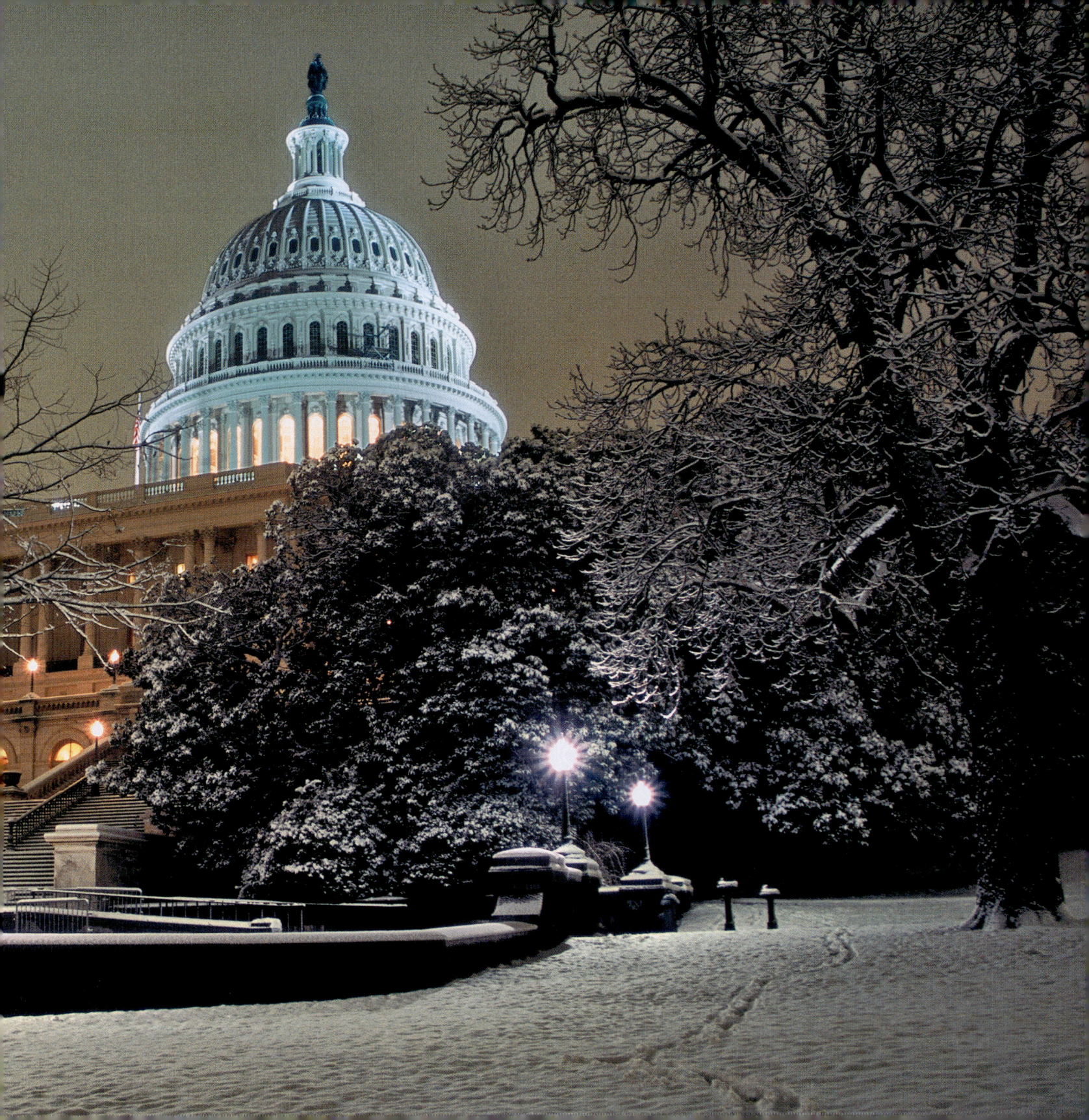

WASHINGTON, D.C., the seat of the United States Federal Government for over 200 years, is arguably the most beautiful city in the United States. A walk through downtown Washington can be like opening an American history book every few steps and reading a page selected at random. Seemingly, around every corner there is some reminder of a prominent person, place, or event from the nation's past. Millions of visitors make pilgrimages every year to these famous landmarks that have become American icons, such as the White House, the Washington Monument, the Jefferson Memorial, and the Lincoln Memorial. Some of the lesser known sites are often overlooked, but are beautiful gems nonetheless, inconspicuously tucked away in nooks and recesses along streets, such as the Einstein Memorial, or in park alcoves, such as the National Arboretum.

The District of Columbia was established by an act of Congress to be the seat of the Federal Government. George Washington was charged with scouting for a location on the Potomac River, and the ten-by-ten mile diamond that he selected 14 miles from his Mount Vernon estate was ceded by the State of Maryland. The area was essentially undeveloped at the time, making it possible for the planners to create an entirely new Federal City from the ground up. The basic plan for the city was conceived in 1791 by Pierre Charles L'Enfant, a Frenchman who had fought in the American Revolutionary Army and had become friends with George Washington. L'Enfant envisioned a monumental core with the two main houses of government, the Congress and the President's Palace (*i.e.*, the White House), on high ground with commanding views and serving as focal points from which broad avenues would radiate diagonally. L'Enfant's plan for the city, now universally regarded as the greatest achievement in American urban planning, was at the time met with horror from landowners and developers. Washington reluctantly fired the headstrong L'Enfant, but L'Enfant's brilliant plan prevailed over the years to come.

Besides its aesthetic beauty and its historic significance, Washington, D.C. boasts a cultural richness unparalleled for a city of its size. The concentration of this cultural wealth is, in part, the result of government efforts to make Washington a national resource of culture for all Americans and an international showcase of the nation as a legitimate world power. For those of us fortunate enough to live in the District, we are beneficiaries of such treasures as the Smithsonian Institution (the largest museum system in the world), the Library of Congress (the largest library in the world), the National Archives, and much more; the list goes on and on. And most of these riches are accessible and free to the public.

Have I convinced you yet that Washington, D.C. is an amazing place? For a photographer, Washington's aesthetic, historical, and cultural elements offer endless opportunities for interesting images. My interest in photography, however, initially grew out of my passion for nature. Indeed, the beauty of nature is often an important element in my photographs: a red Harvest Moon rising over the National Mall, or spring blossoms around the Washington Monument in the morning twilight. For me, photography is about life and capturing the light during magical moments. I hope you will enjoy the images in this book as much as I've enjoyed experiencing the magical moments they represent.

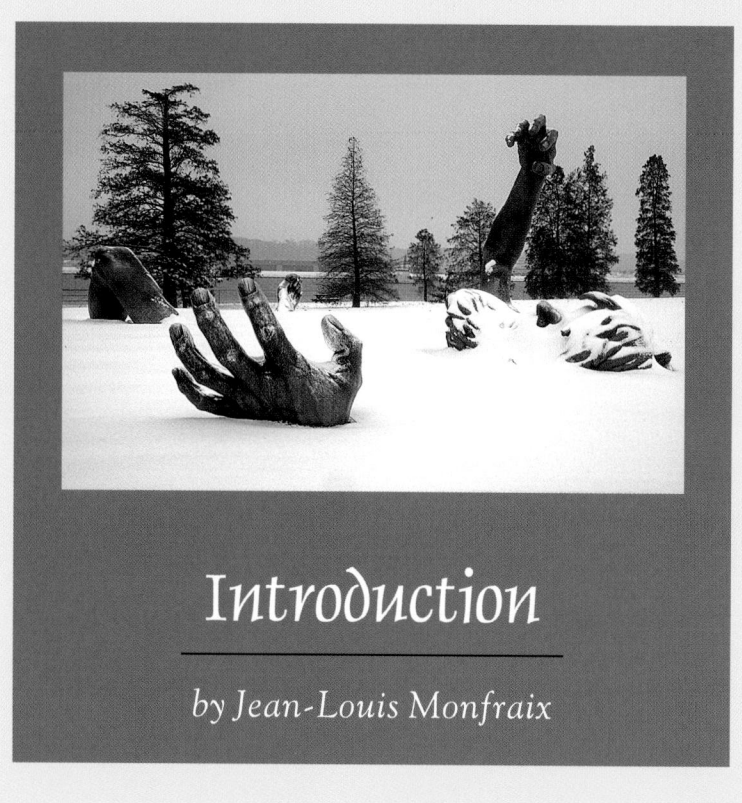

Introduction

by Jean-Louis Monfraix

To my wife Cynthia, who has stood by me through my metamorphosis from musician, to biologist, to photographer. Without her love and support, the journey would never have been possible.

"The Awakening", a statue by J. Seward Johnson, under a fresh blanket of snow at Hains Point.

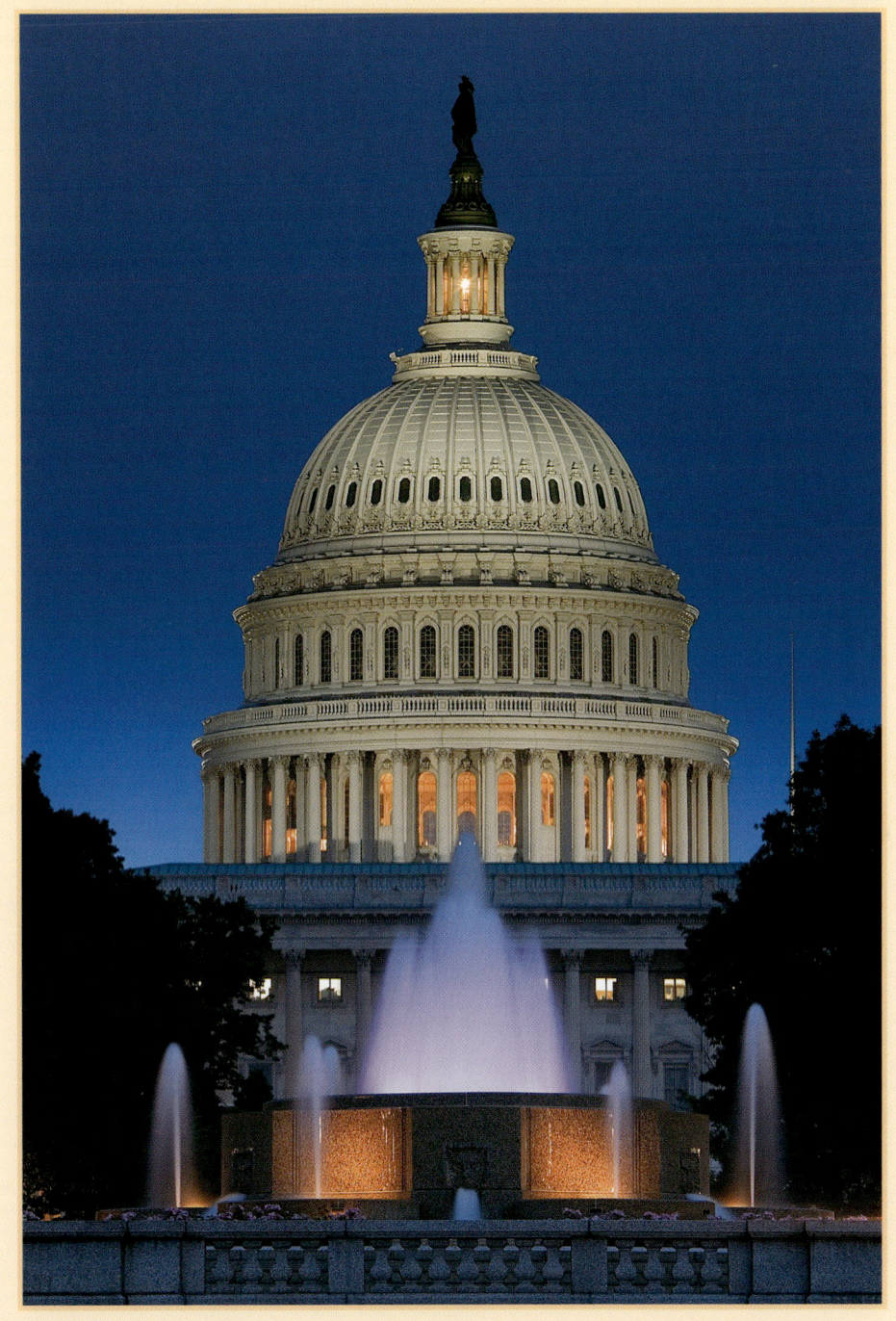

Twilight brings gorgeous colors to the Capitol Dome. The House of Representatives is in session as dusk settles, revealing the changing colors of the fountain

SUNRISE OVER the grounds of the Netherlands Carillon, with a view of the Washington, D.C. skyline in the background. The Carillon, located in Virginia, was a gift from the Dutch people for American aid received during and after World War II.

Next pages: Night-time and sunrise views of the Marine Corps War Memorial, located in Virginia across the Potomac River from D.C. This memorial recreates a famous scene from World War II, when U.S servicemen raised an American flag on the top of Mount Suribachi during the struggle for the island of Iwo Jima.

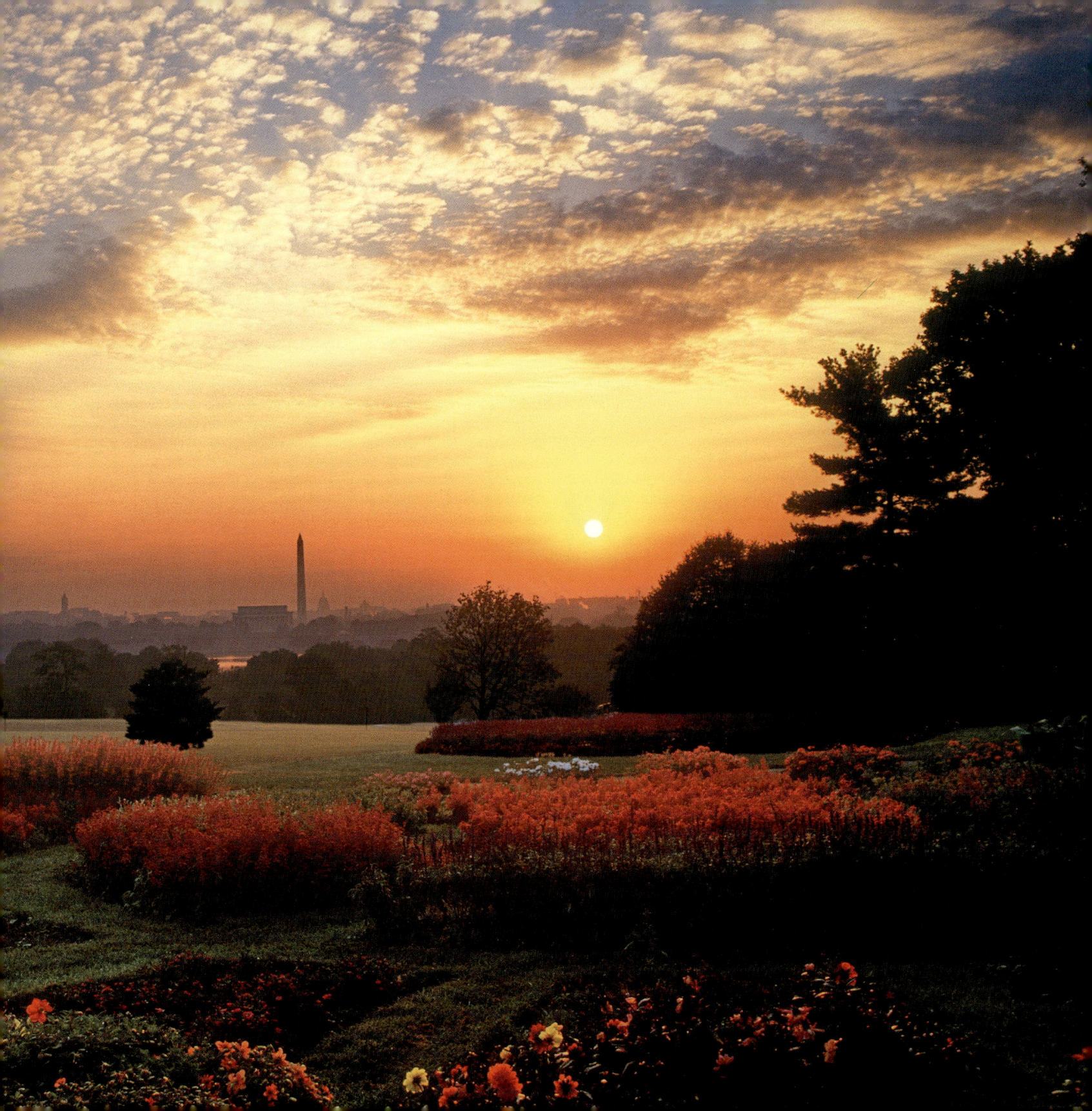

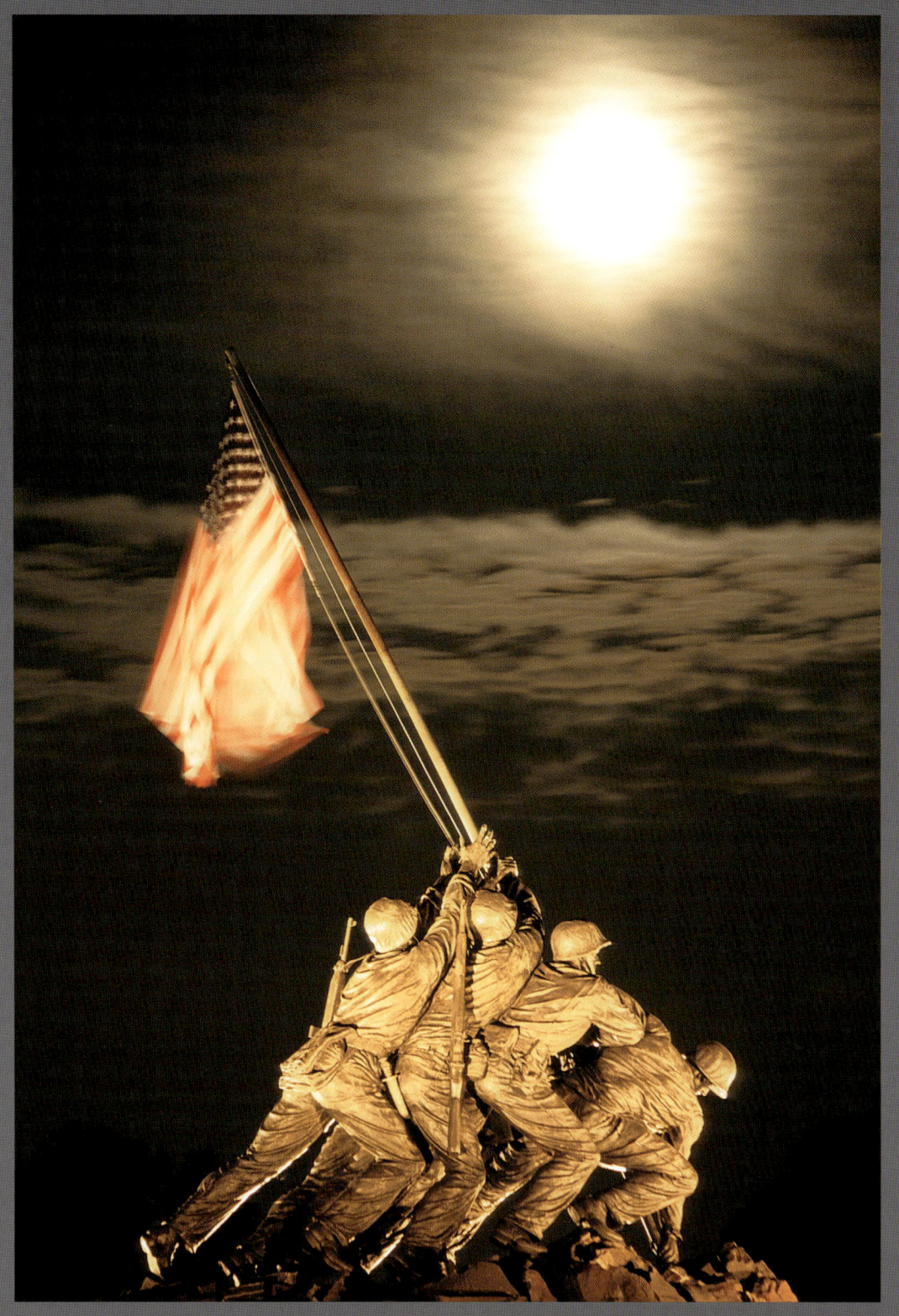

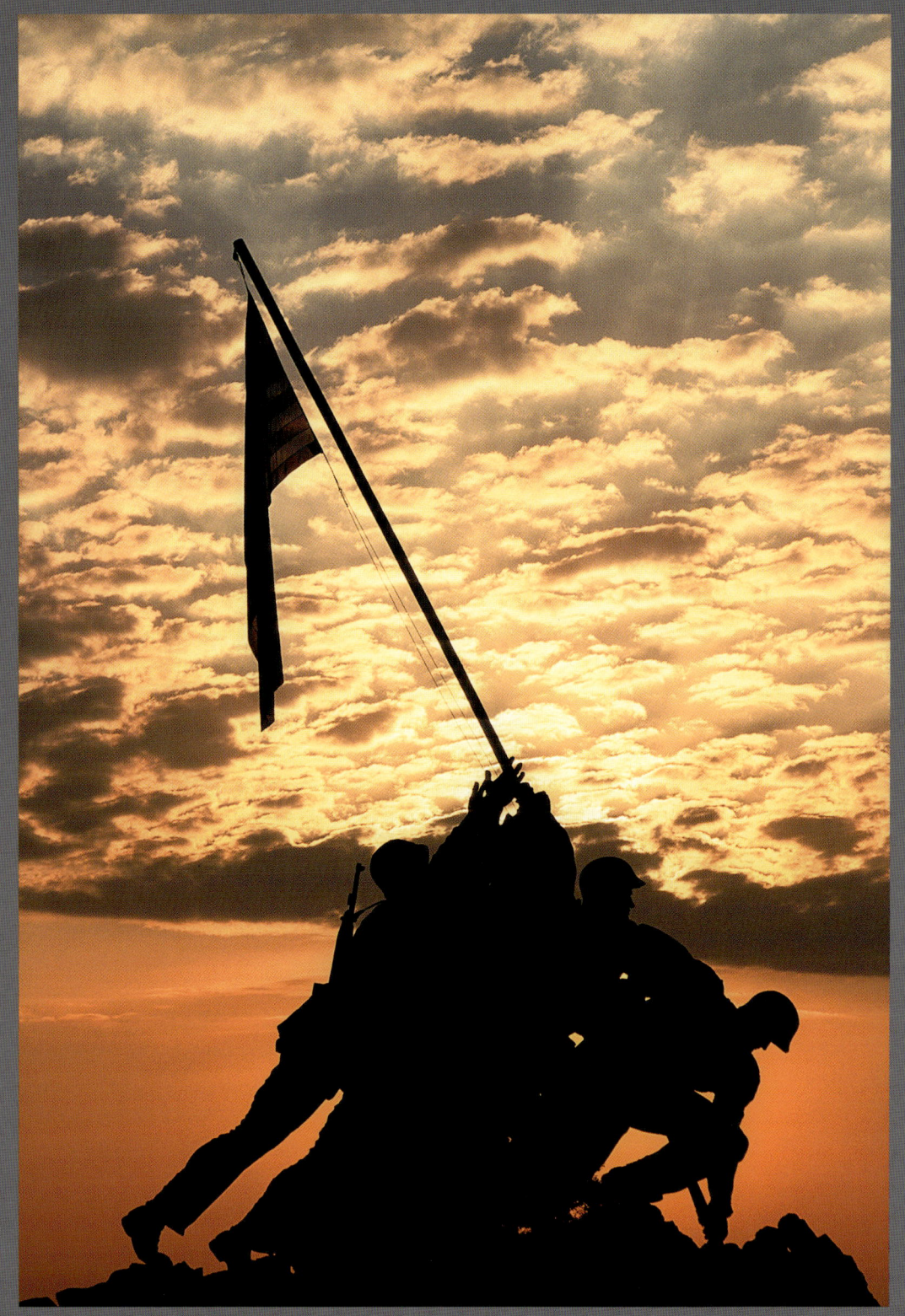

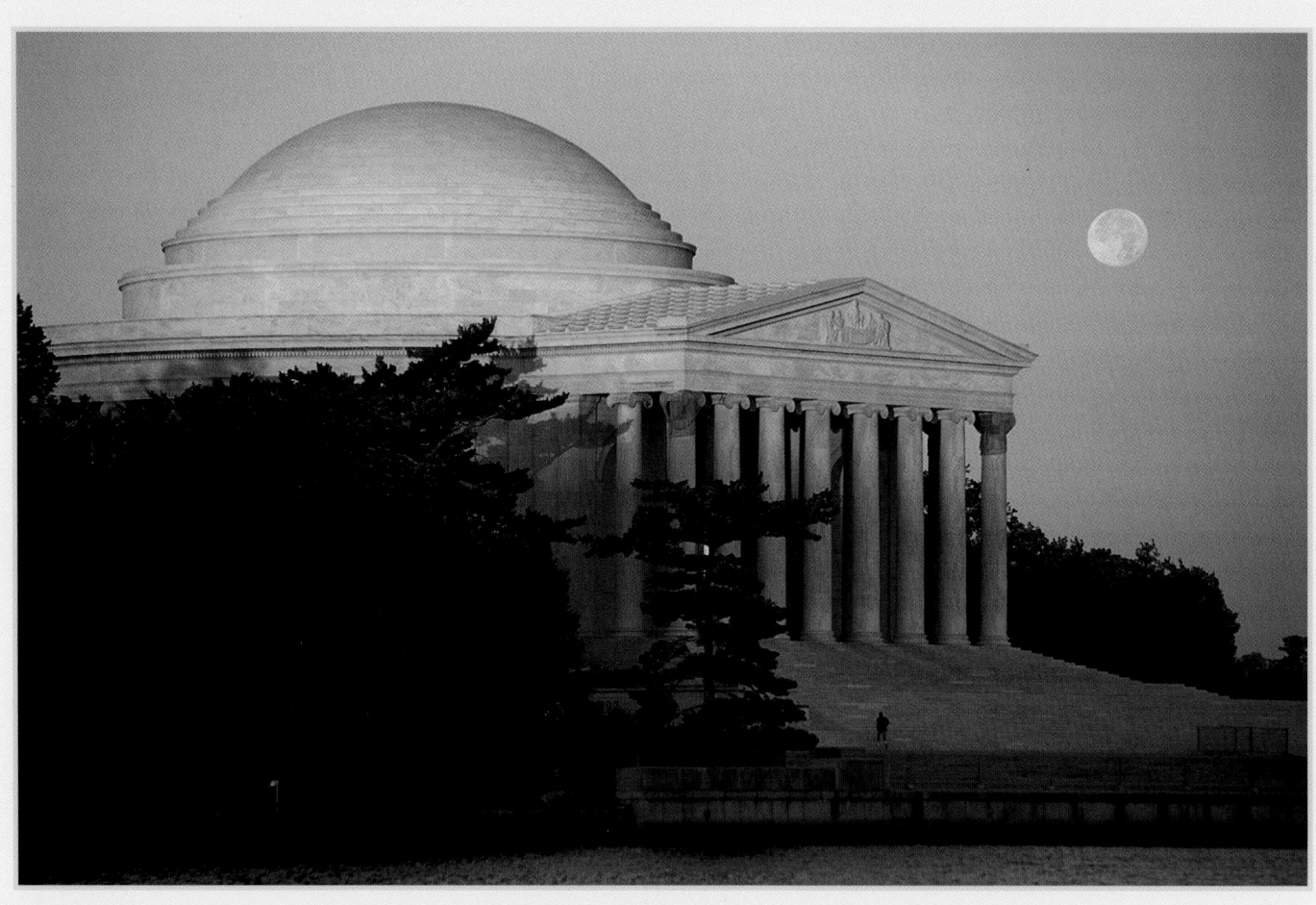

A full moon sets over the Thomas Jefferson Memorial.

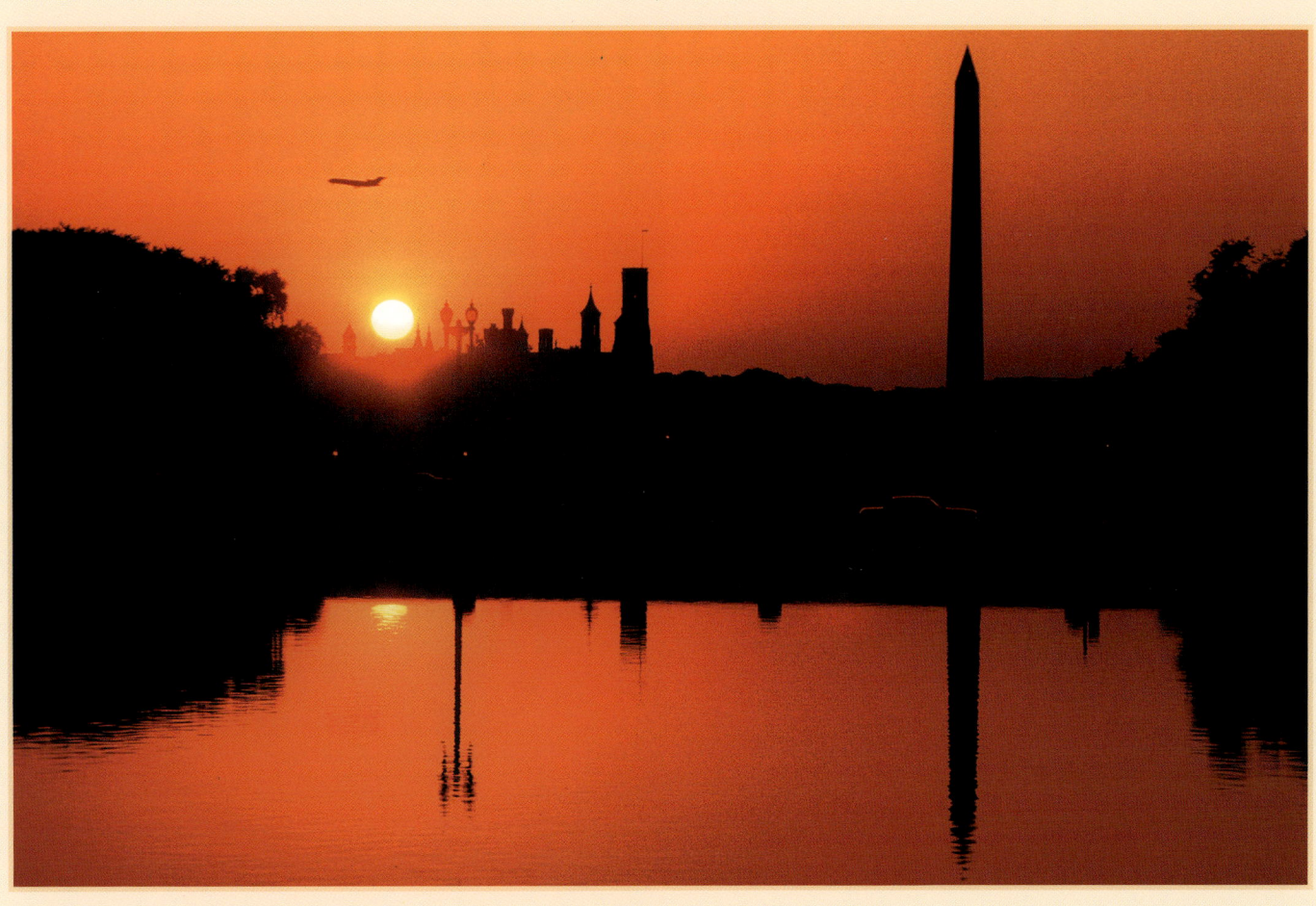

A red sunset over the National Mall is mirrored in the
Capitol Reflecting Pool.

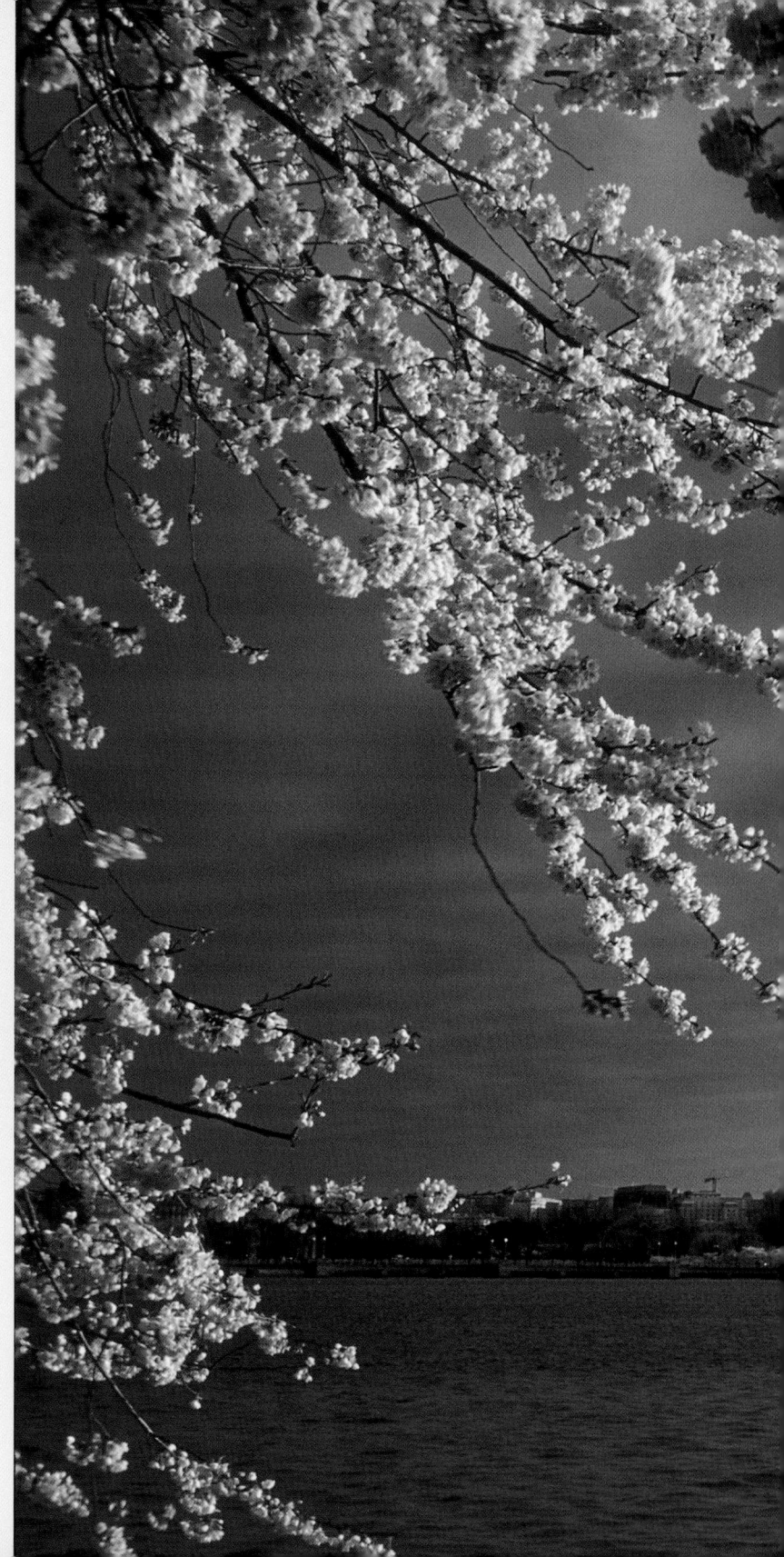

YOSHINO CHERRY TREES, a gift from the city of Tokyo in 1912, line the Tidal Basin of the Thomas Jefferson Memorial. Every spring, thousands of visitors come to D.C. to watch the cherry trees bloom in a beautiful display of pink and white blossoms. This image captures a view of the blossoms framing the Washington Monument.

Next pages: Autumn colors surround the Korean War Veterans Memorial.

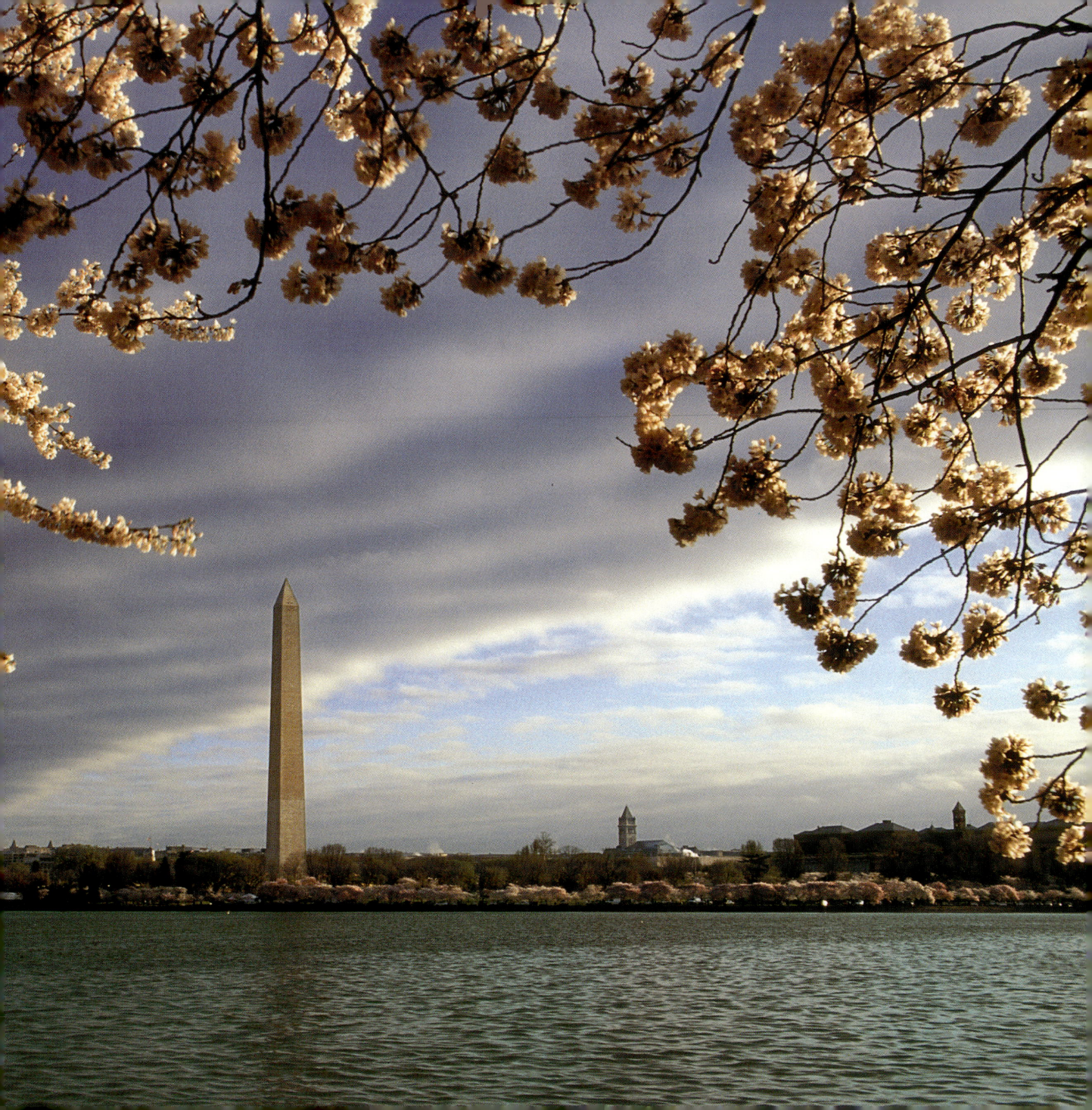

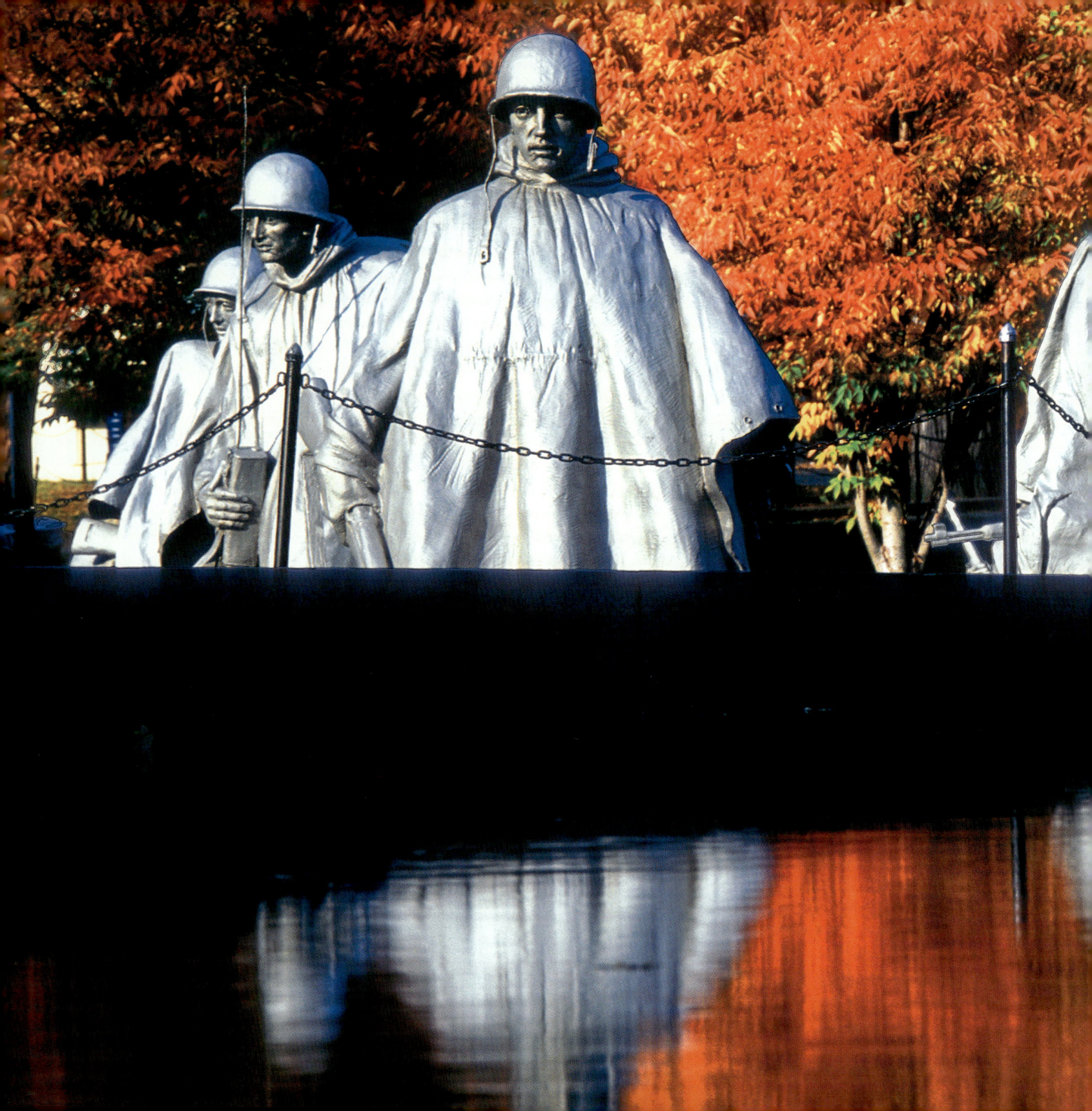

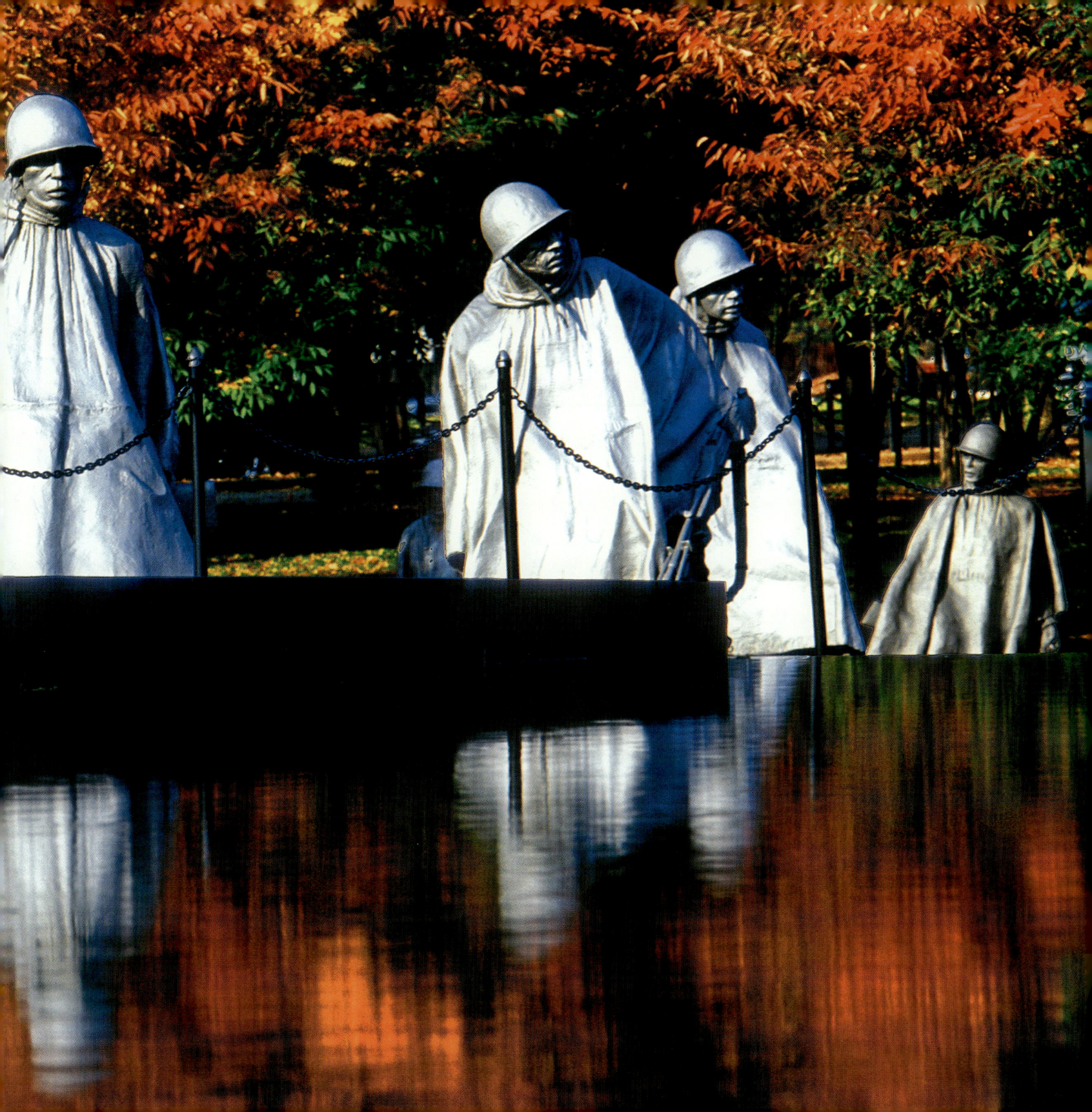

MORNING MIST filters sunrise light on the Chesapeake & Ohio Canal, which follows the route of the Potomac River for 185 miles from Washington, D.C. to Cumberland, Maryland.

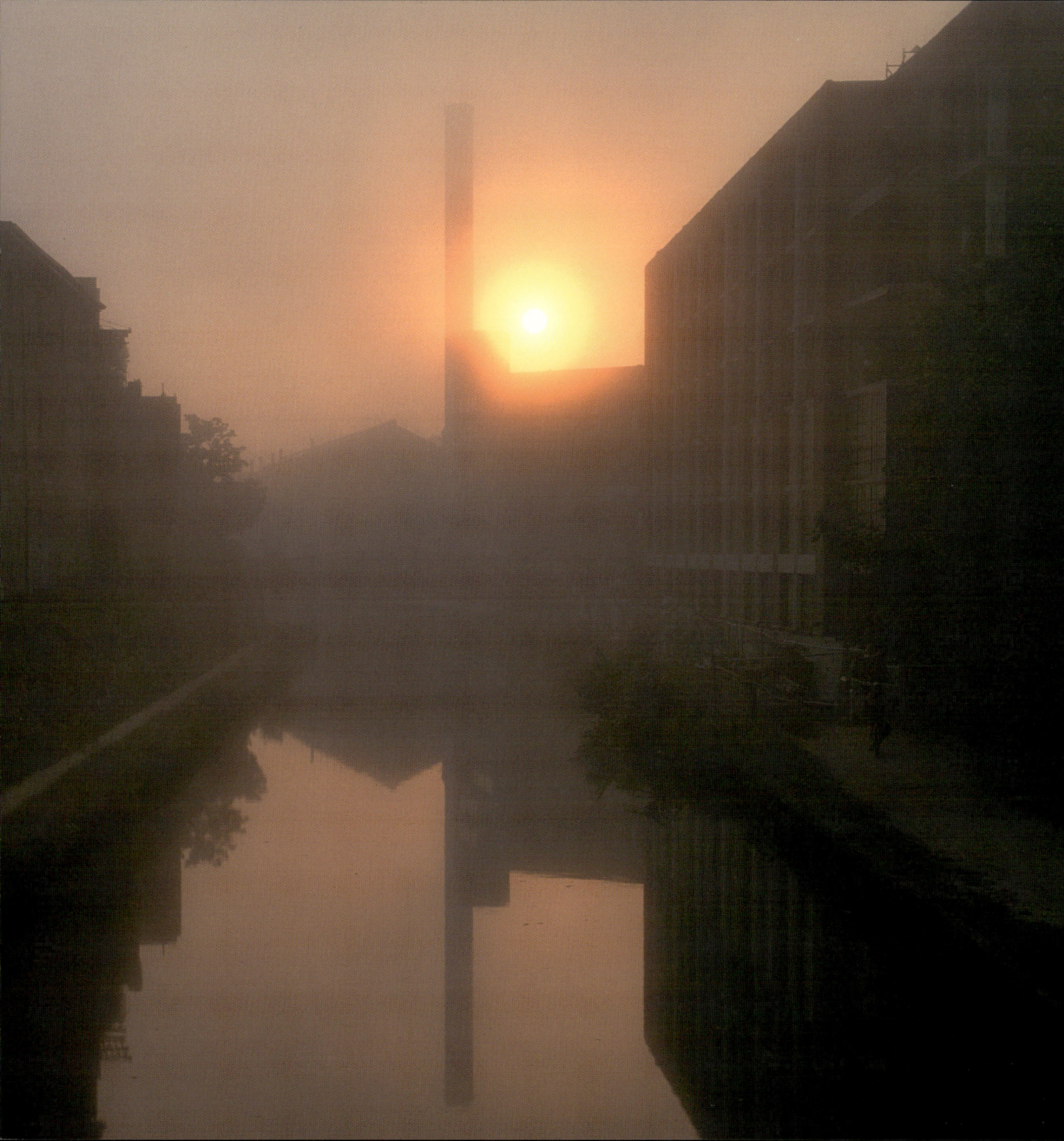

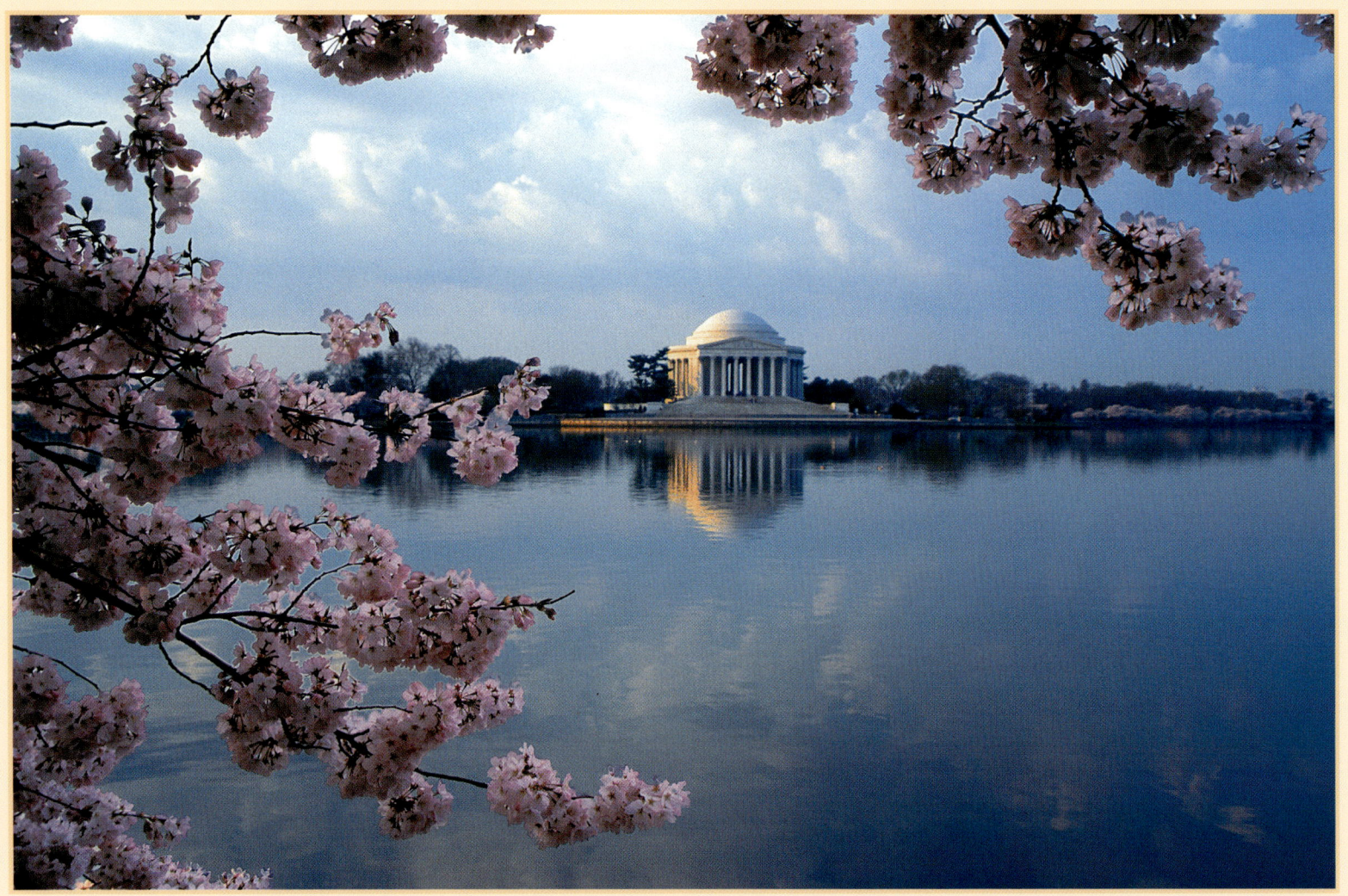

Above: Cherry blossoms frame the Thomas Jefferson Memorial.

Right: In the twilight glow before dawn on a quiet morning, cherry blossoms frame the Washington Monument and its reflection in the unusually placid water of the Tidal Basin.

Next page: A total lunar eclipse over Washington, D.C., as viewed from the Netherlands Carillon in Arlington, Virginia. This is a multiple exposure on a single frame of film.

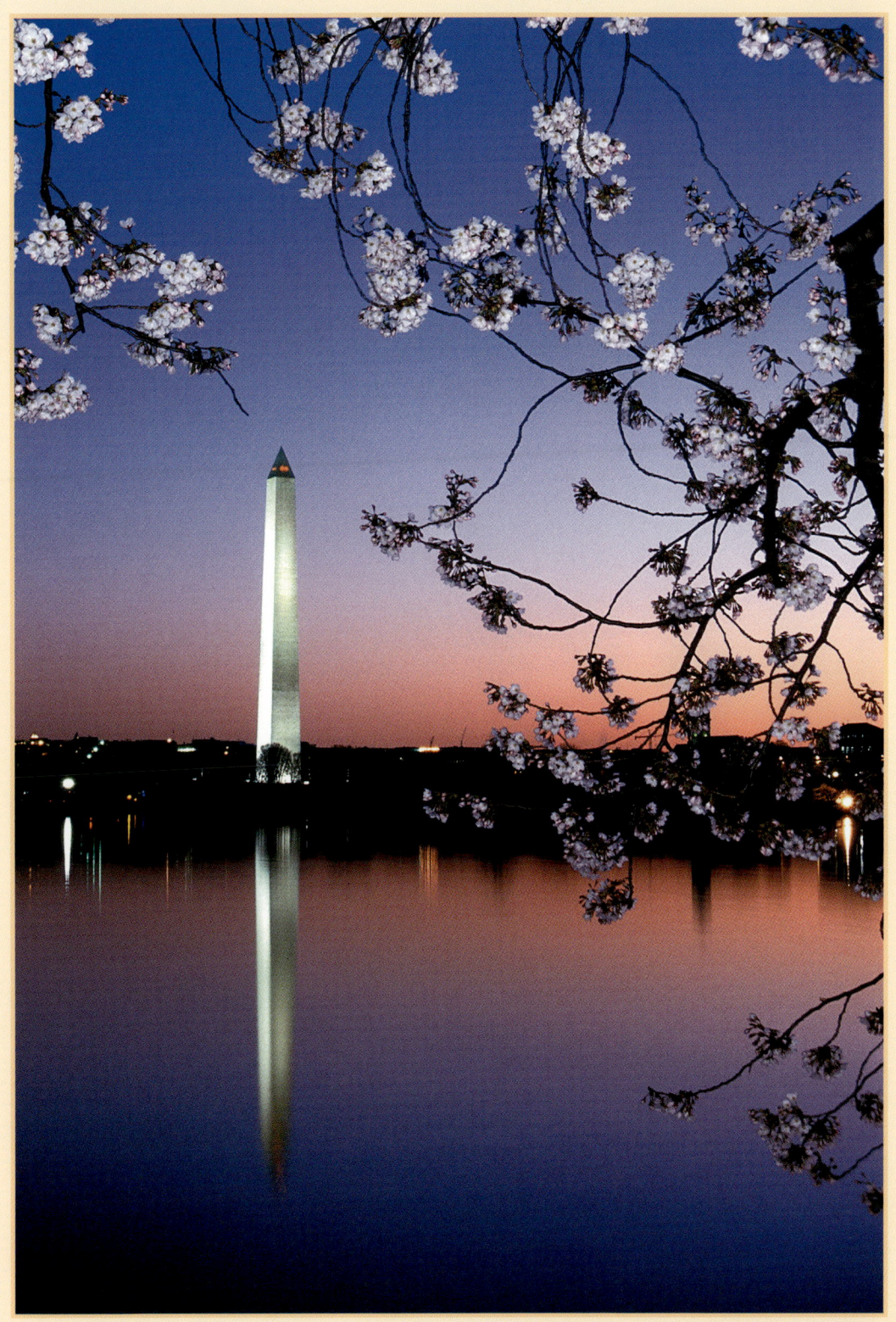

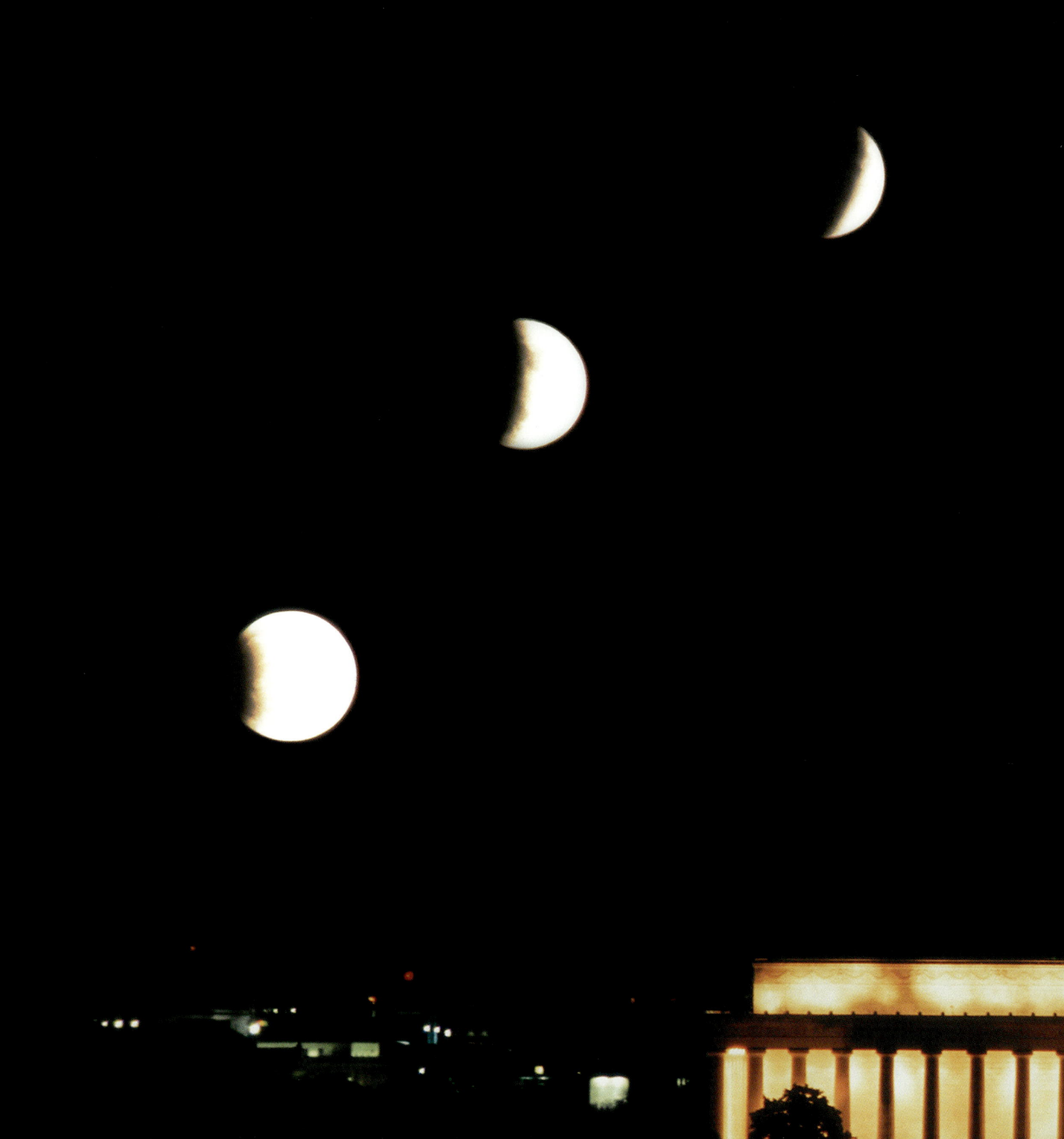

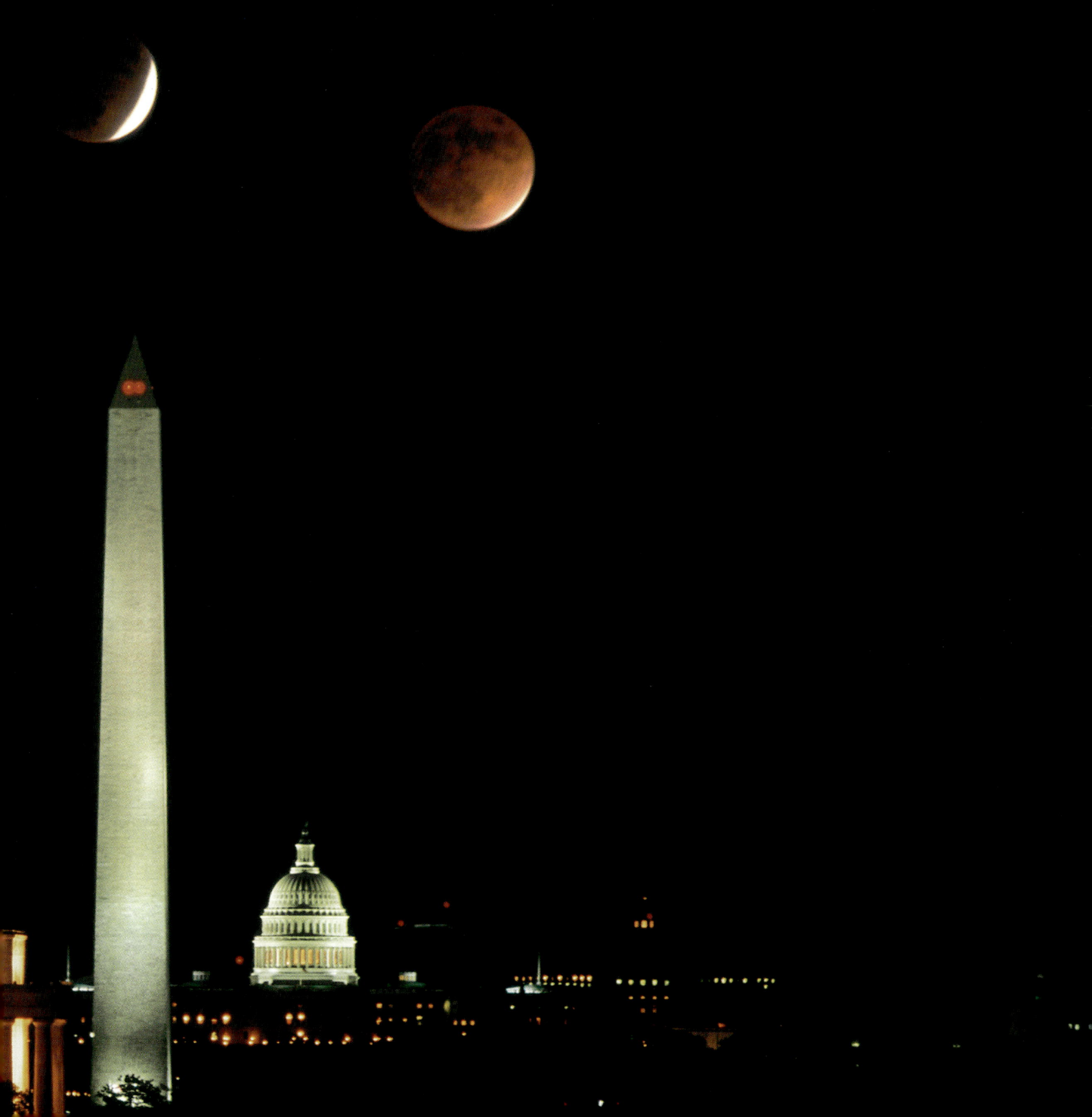

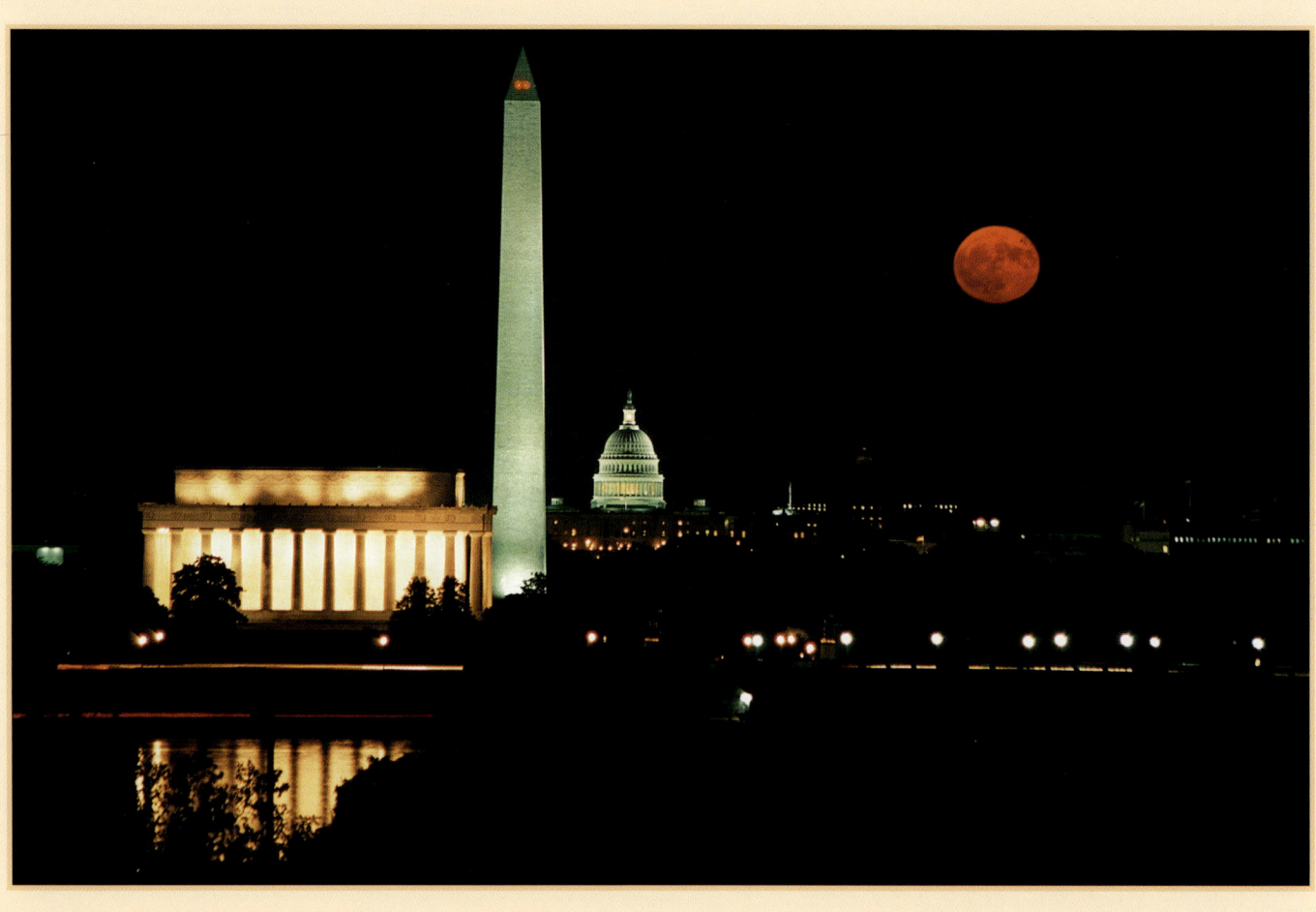

A red harvest moon rises over the Lincoln Memorial, the Washington Monument, and the Capitol Dome.

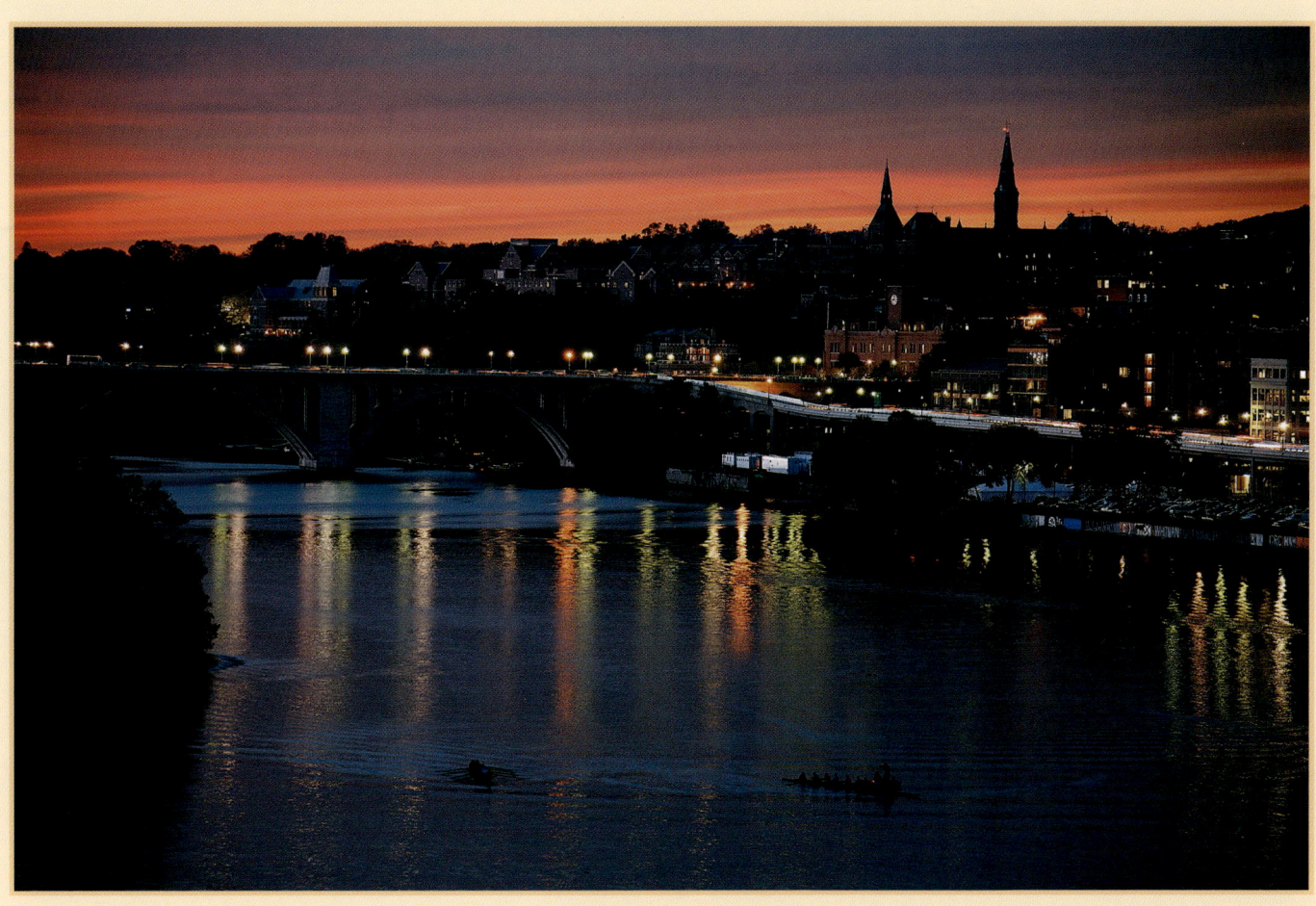

Twilight descends over the Potomac River. Georgetown can be seen on the far side of the river.

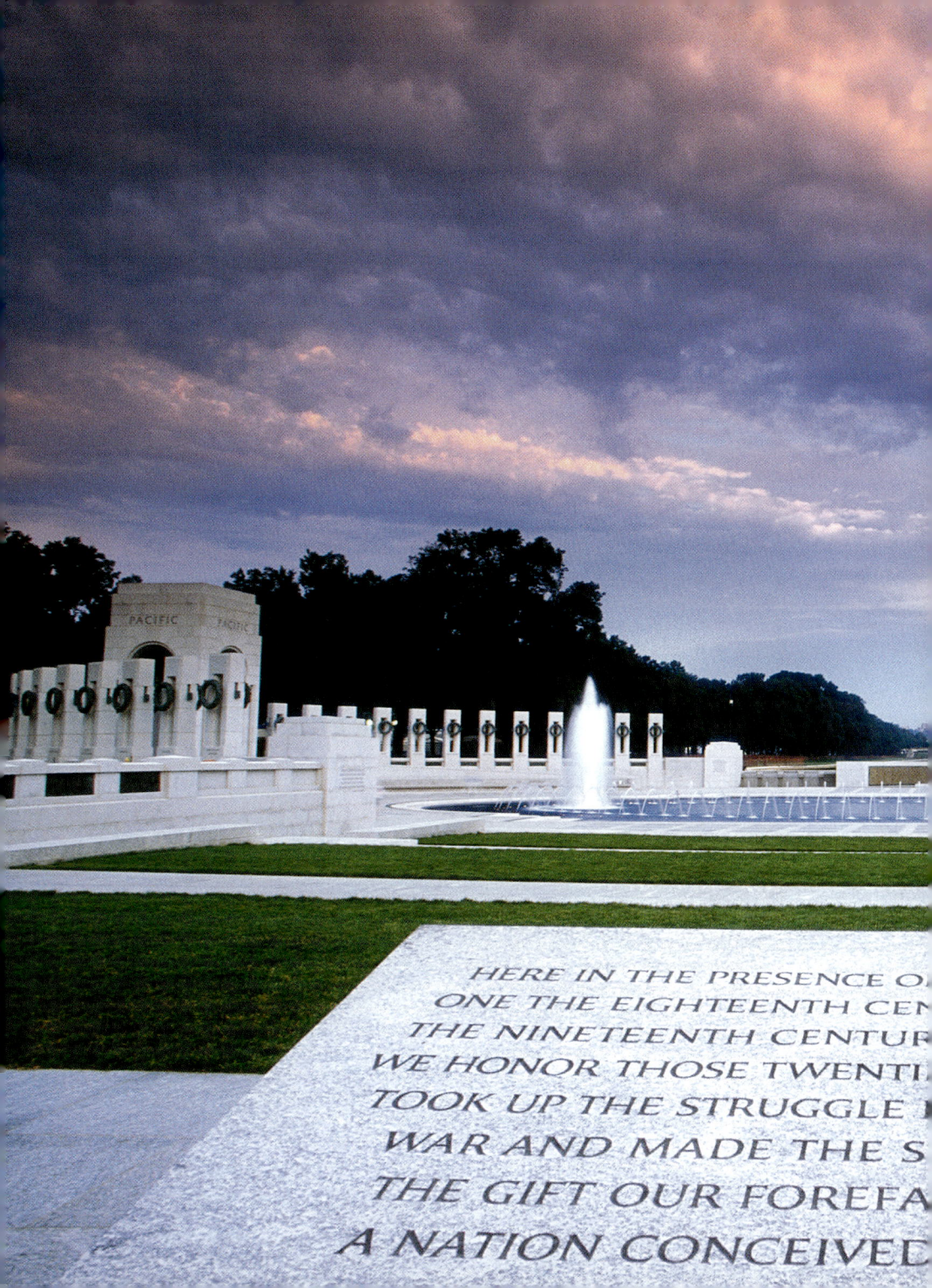

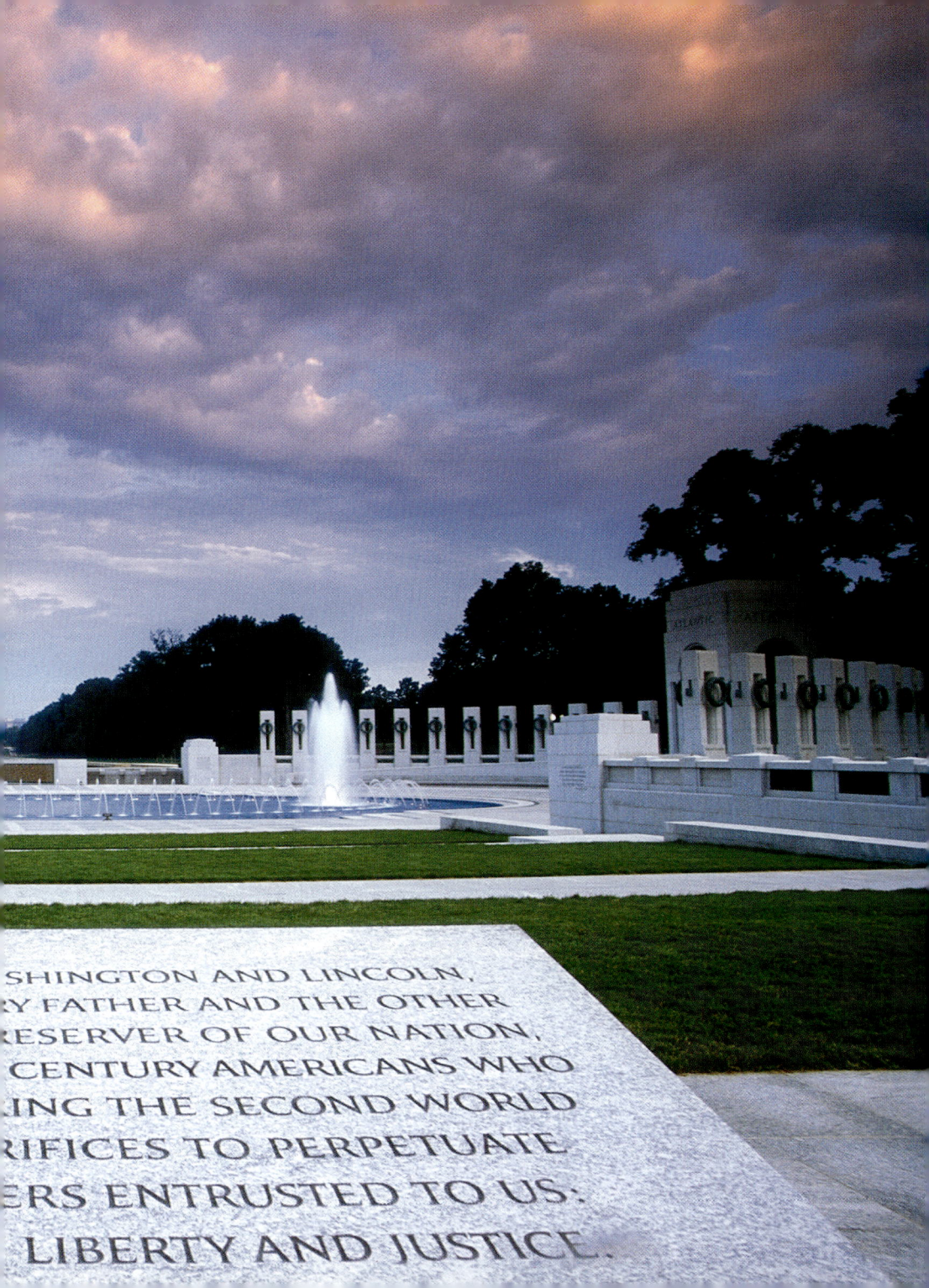

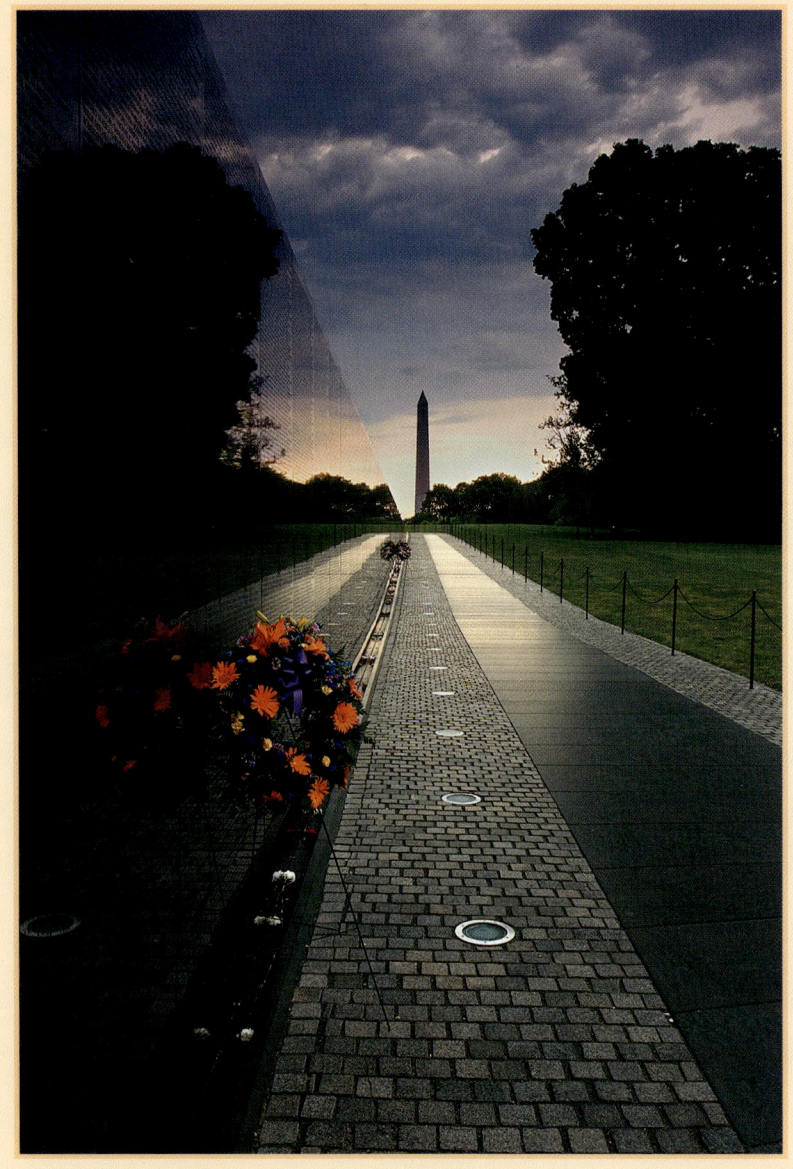

Previous page: The World War II Memorial at sunrise.

Above: The Vietnam Veterans Memorial Wall, photographed at dawn so that the wall would act like a mirror to create this striking symmetry.

Right: "The Three Servicemen," part of the Vietnam Veterans Memorial.

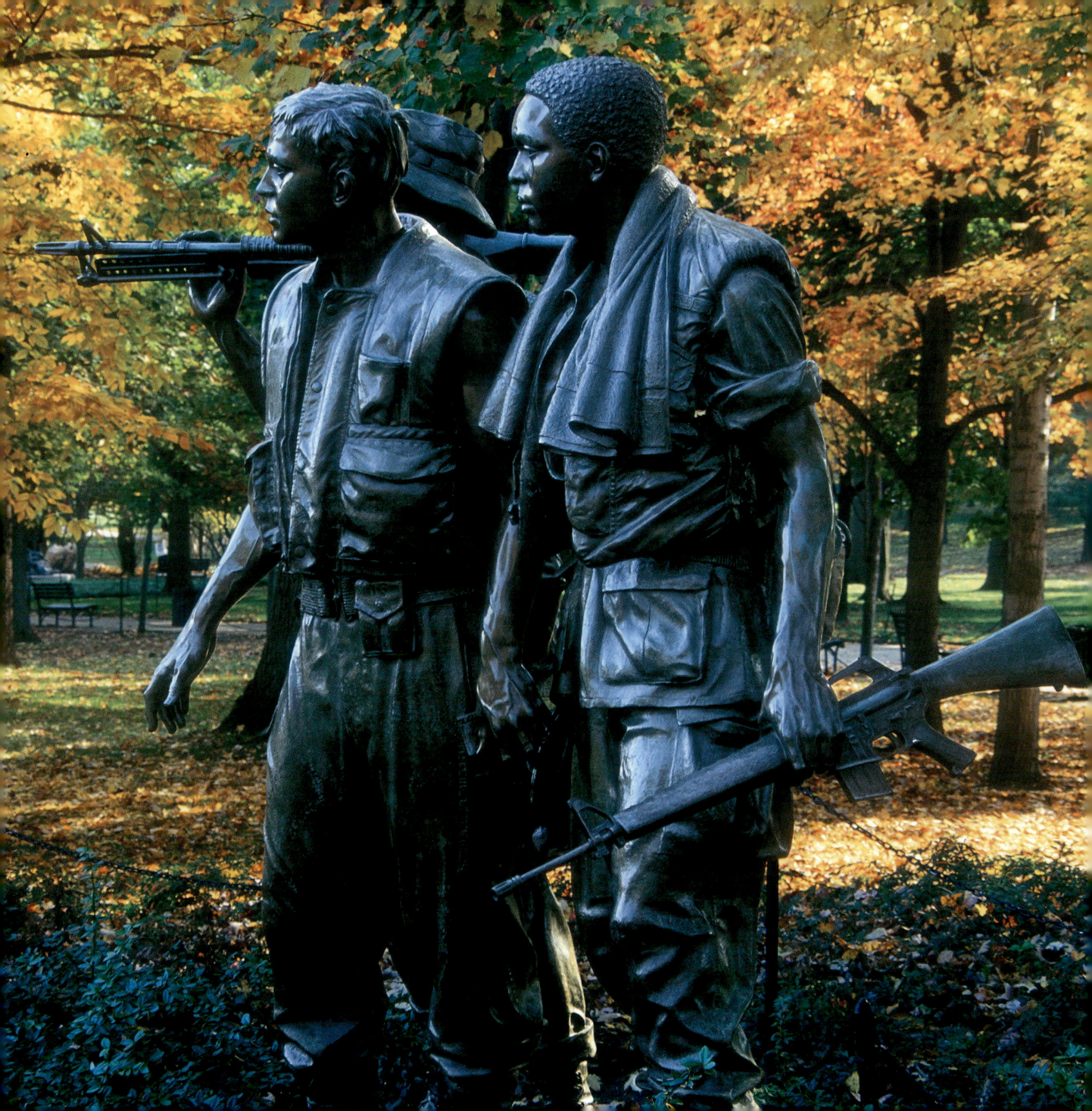

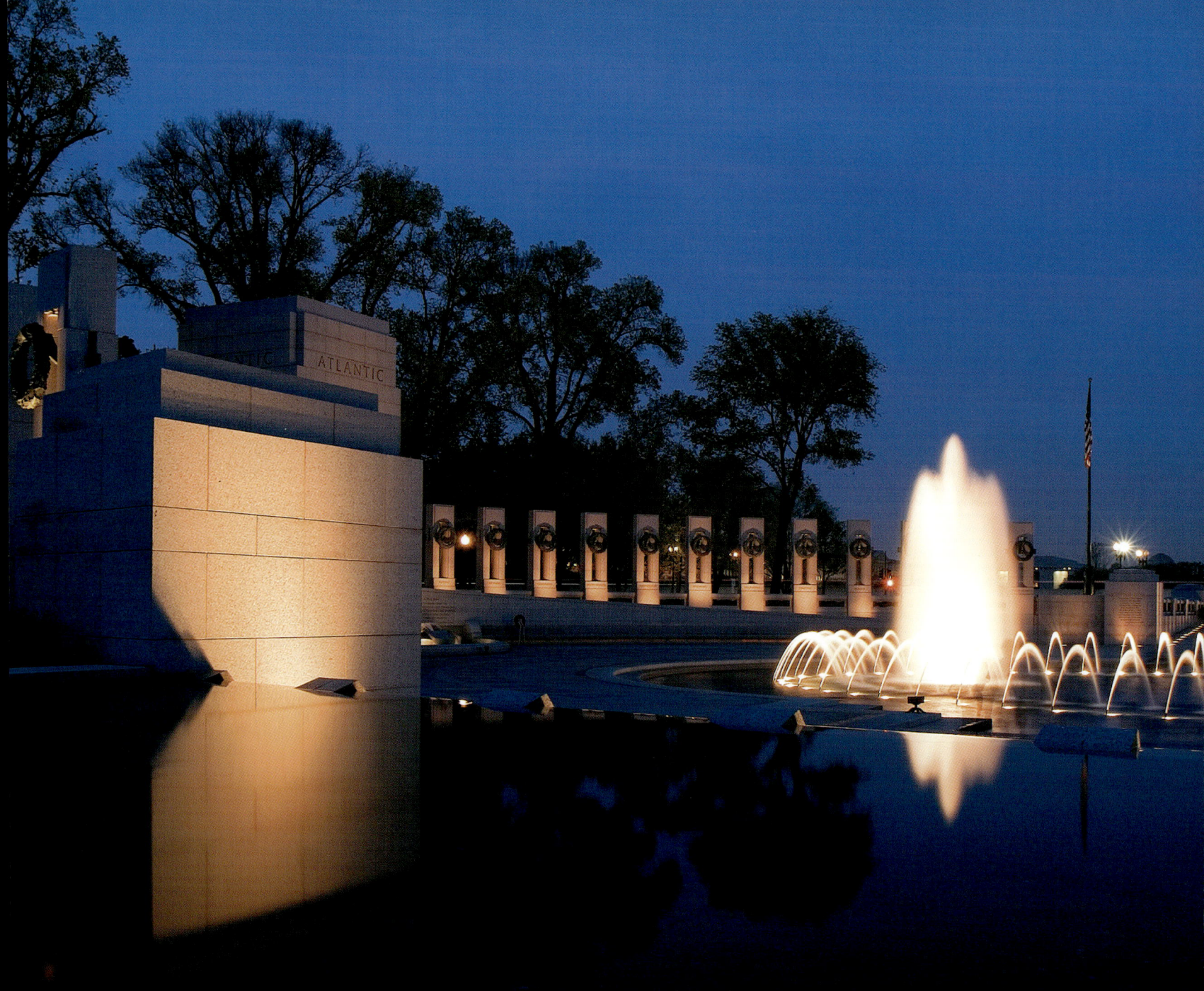

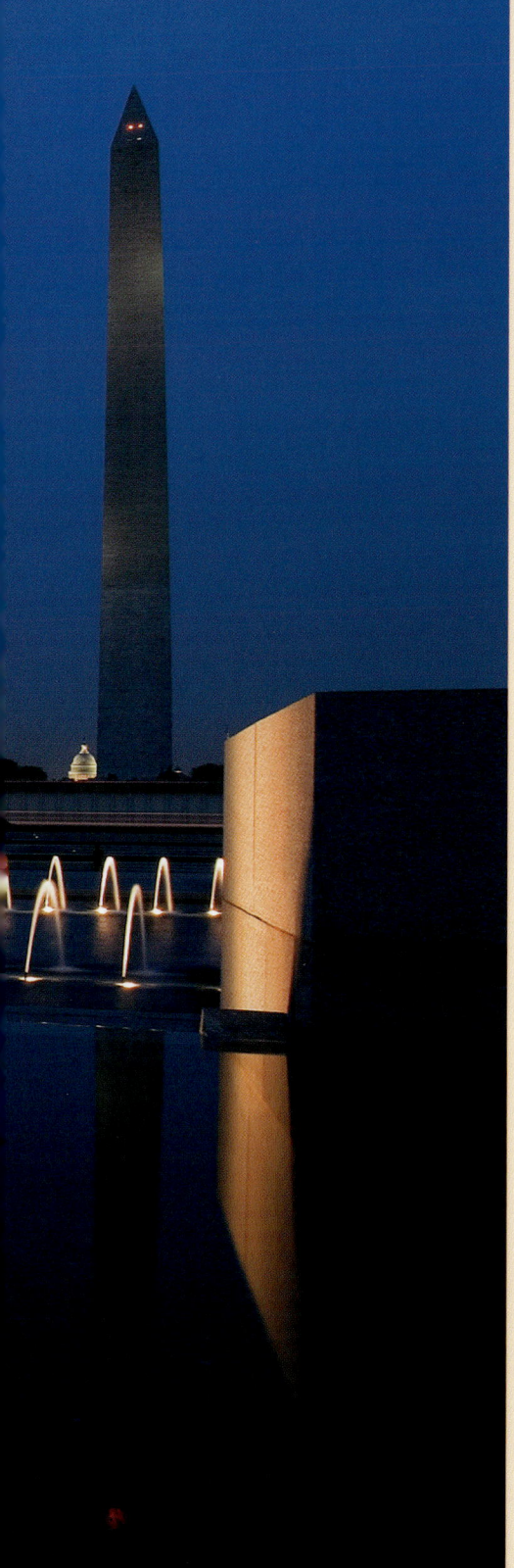

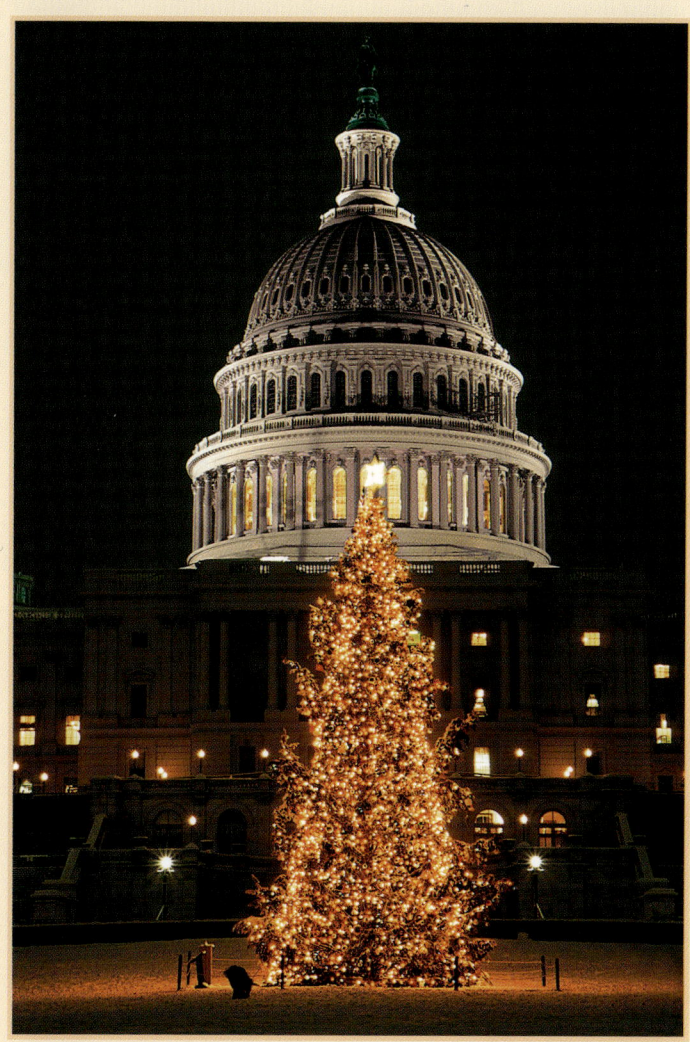

D USK VIEW of the World War II Memorial. The Memorial honors the 16 million who served in the armed forces of the United States, and the more than 400,000 who died.

Above: Every year a tree is placed on the Capitol grounds and decorated in celebration of the holiday season.

SOUTHWEST D.C.'S waterfront lights up with the coming of night.

Next pages: A view of the Lincoln Memorial and the Arlington Memorial Bridge from Arlington House (The Robert E. Lee Memorial). Widely regarded as the most beautiful bridge in Washington, the Memorial Bridge links the Lincoln Memorial in the District of Columbia to Arlington National Cemetery in Virginia.

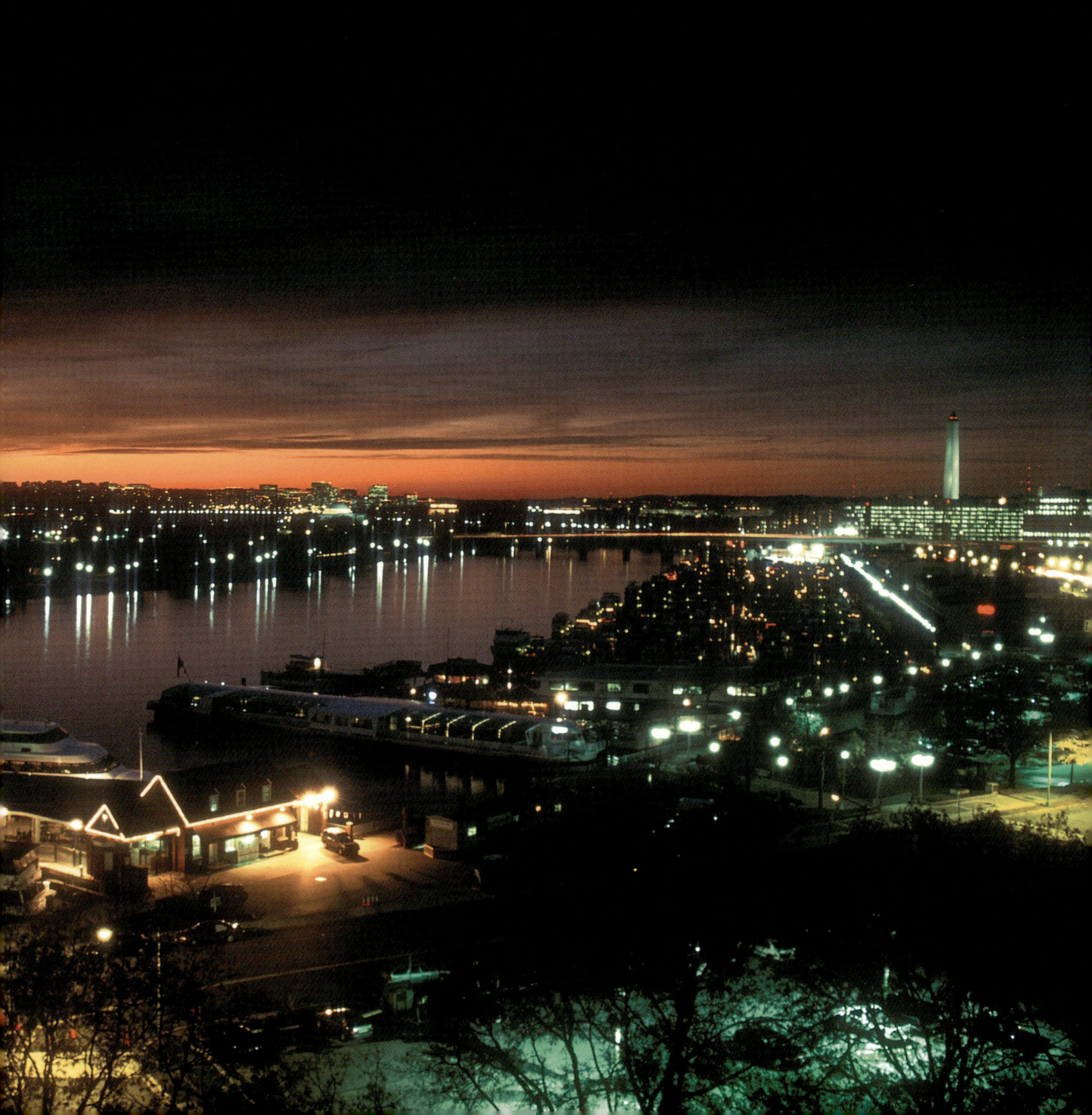

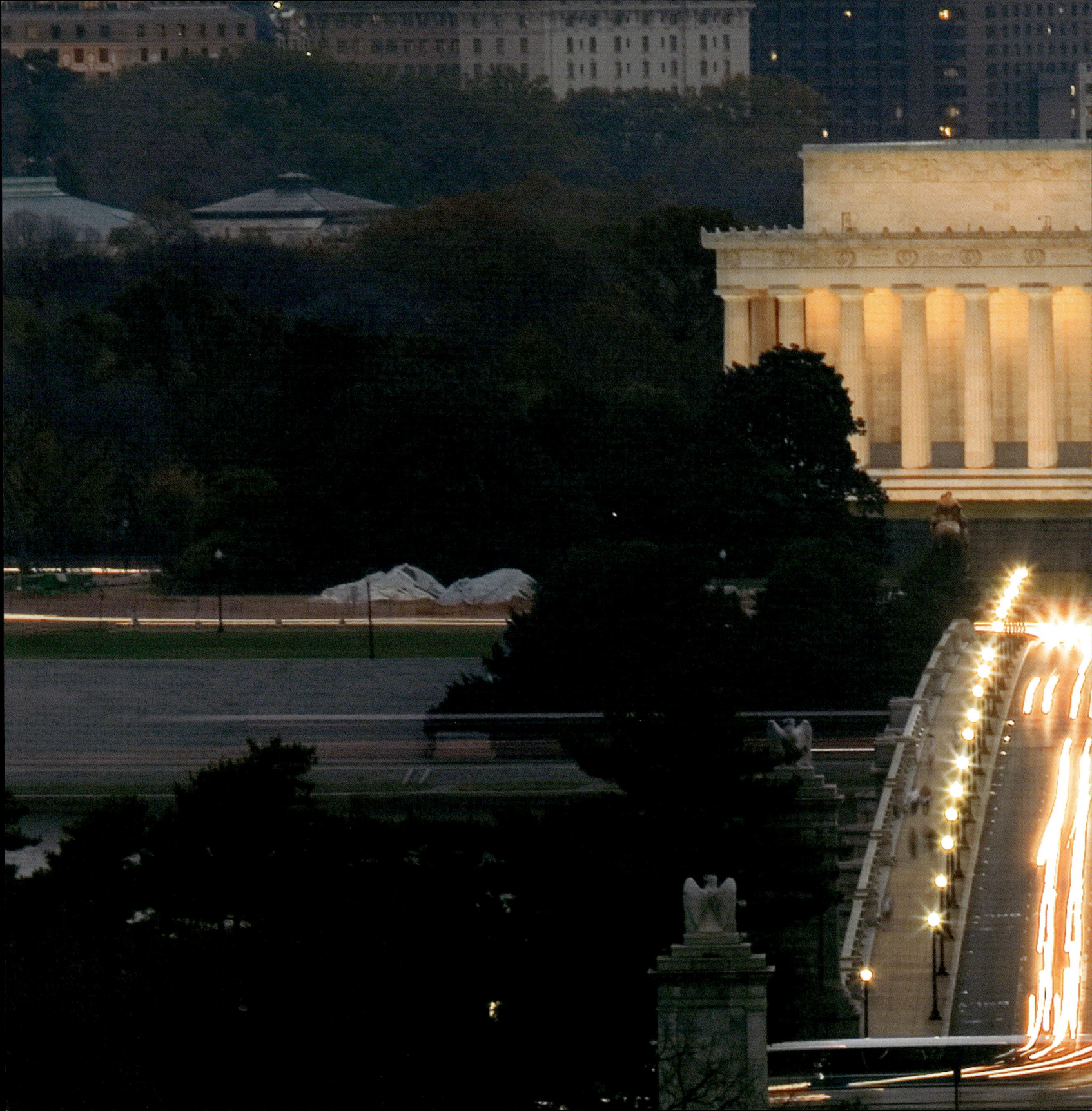

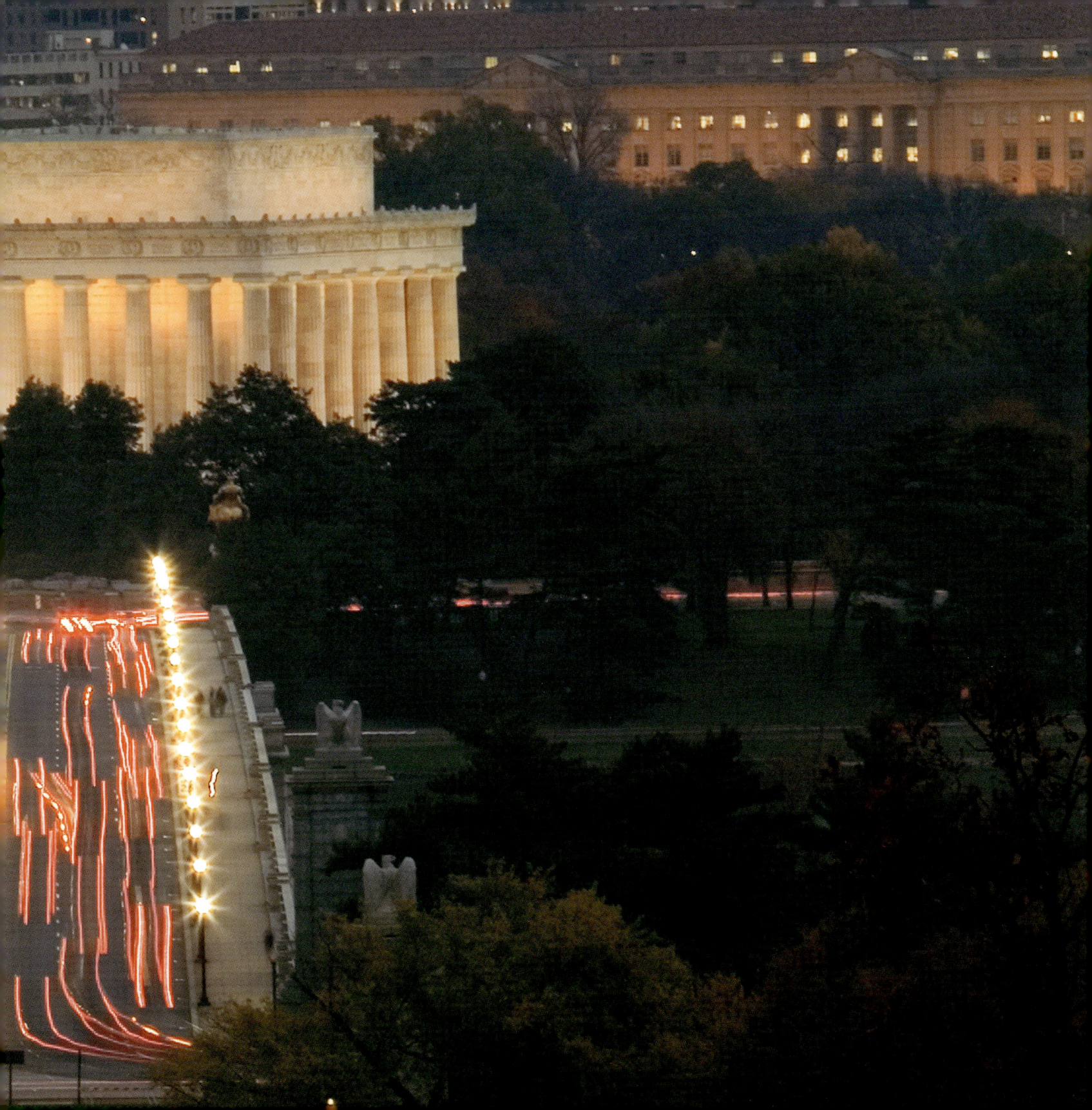

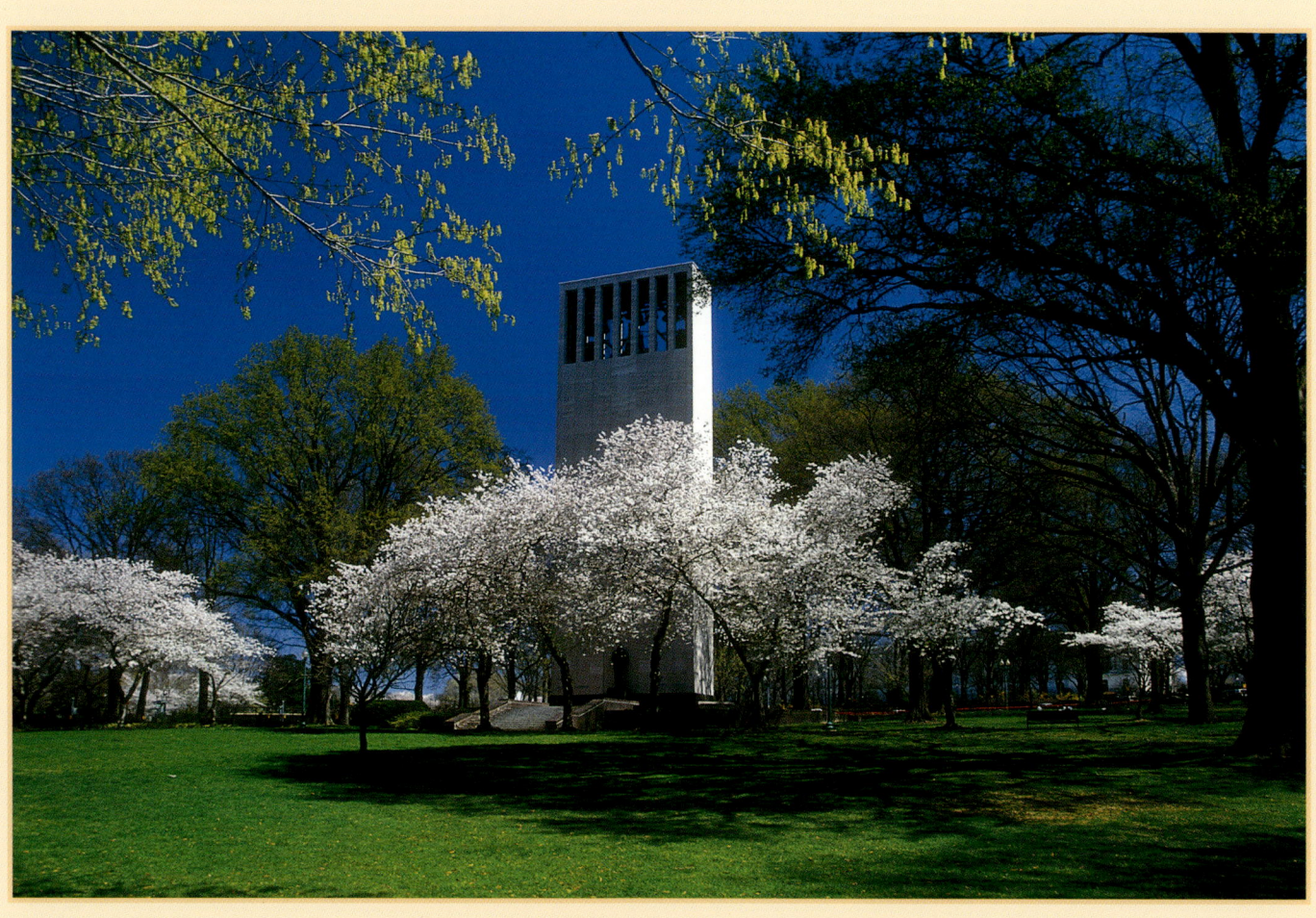

Cherry trees bloom in early April below the Robert A. Taft Memorial and Carillon. Robert A. Taft, son of President William H. Taft, served in the Senate from 1939 to 1953.

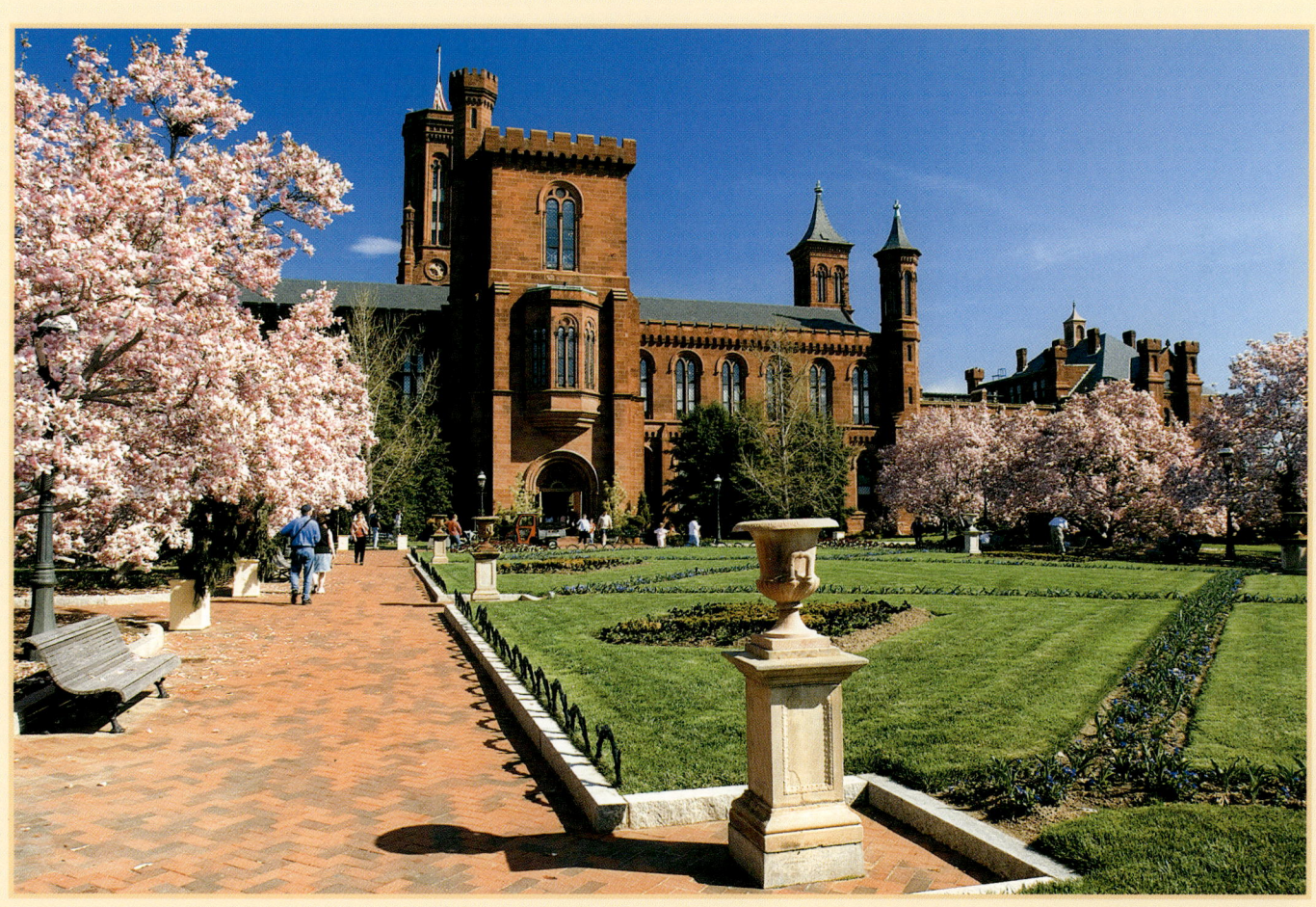

Spring magnolia blossoms in the Enid A. Haupt Garden and the famous Smithsonian Castle.

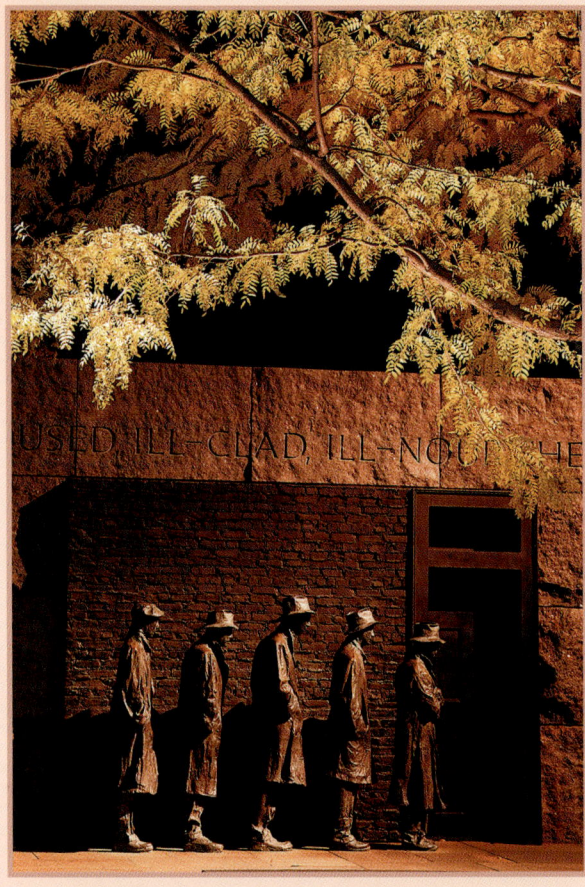

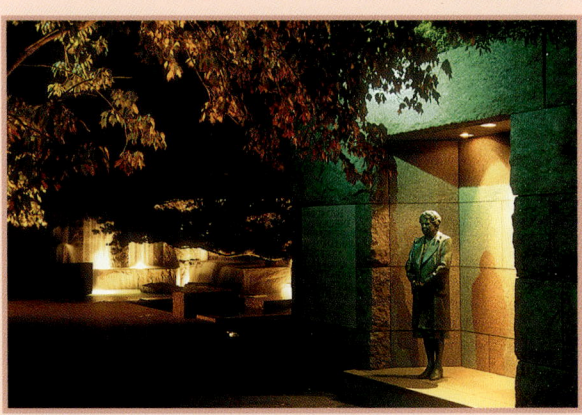

THREE NIGHTTIME VIEWS of the Franklin Delano Roosevelt Memorial. Located along the Cherry Tree Walk on the western edge of the Tidal Basin near the Jefferson Memorial, this memorial remembers our 32nd president and the challenges faced by the nation during his time in office.

Next pages: Dusk settles over the National Cathedral.

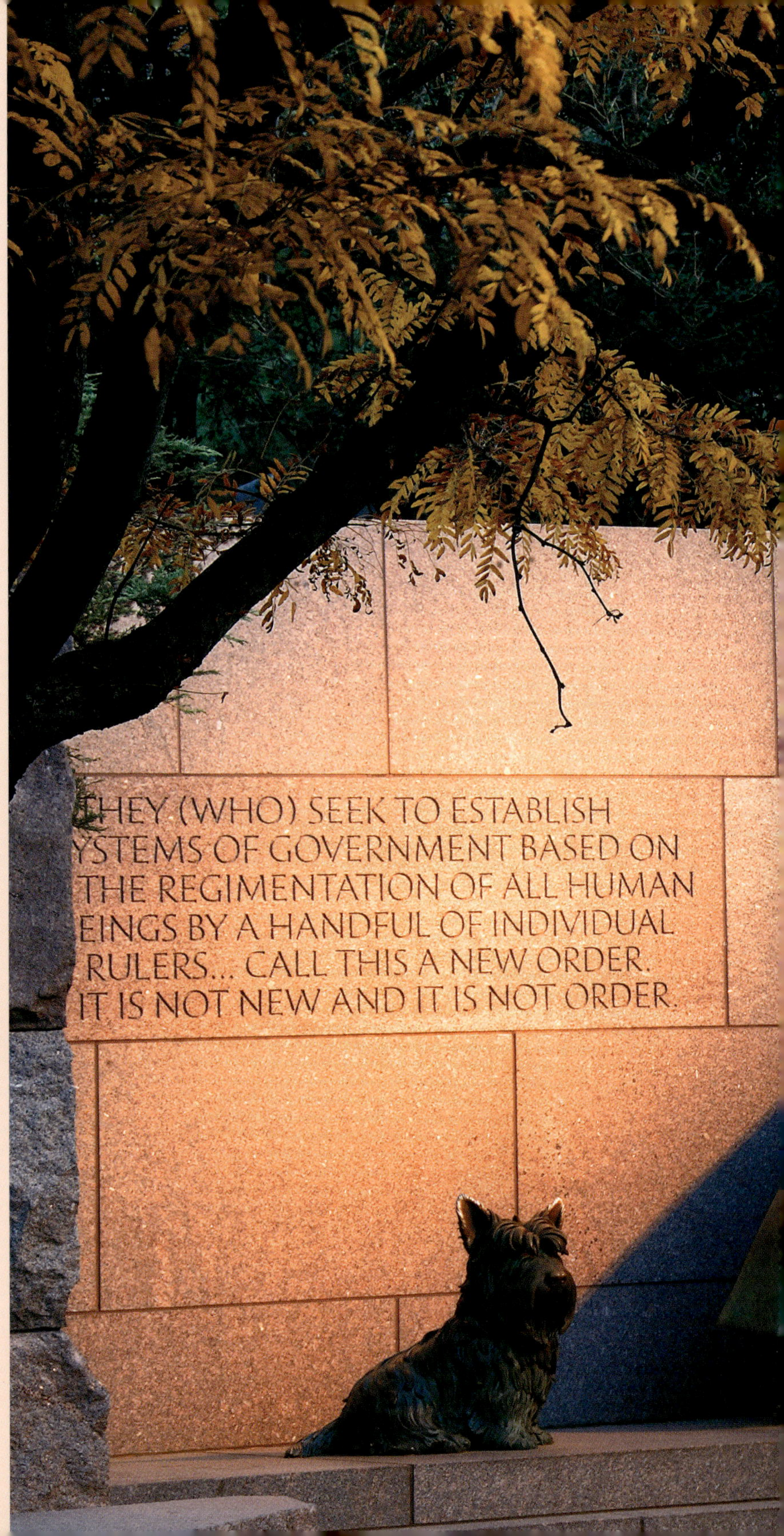

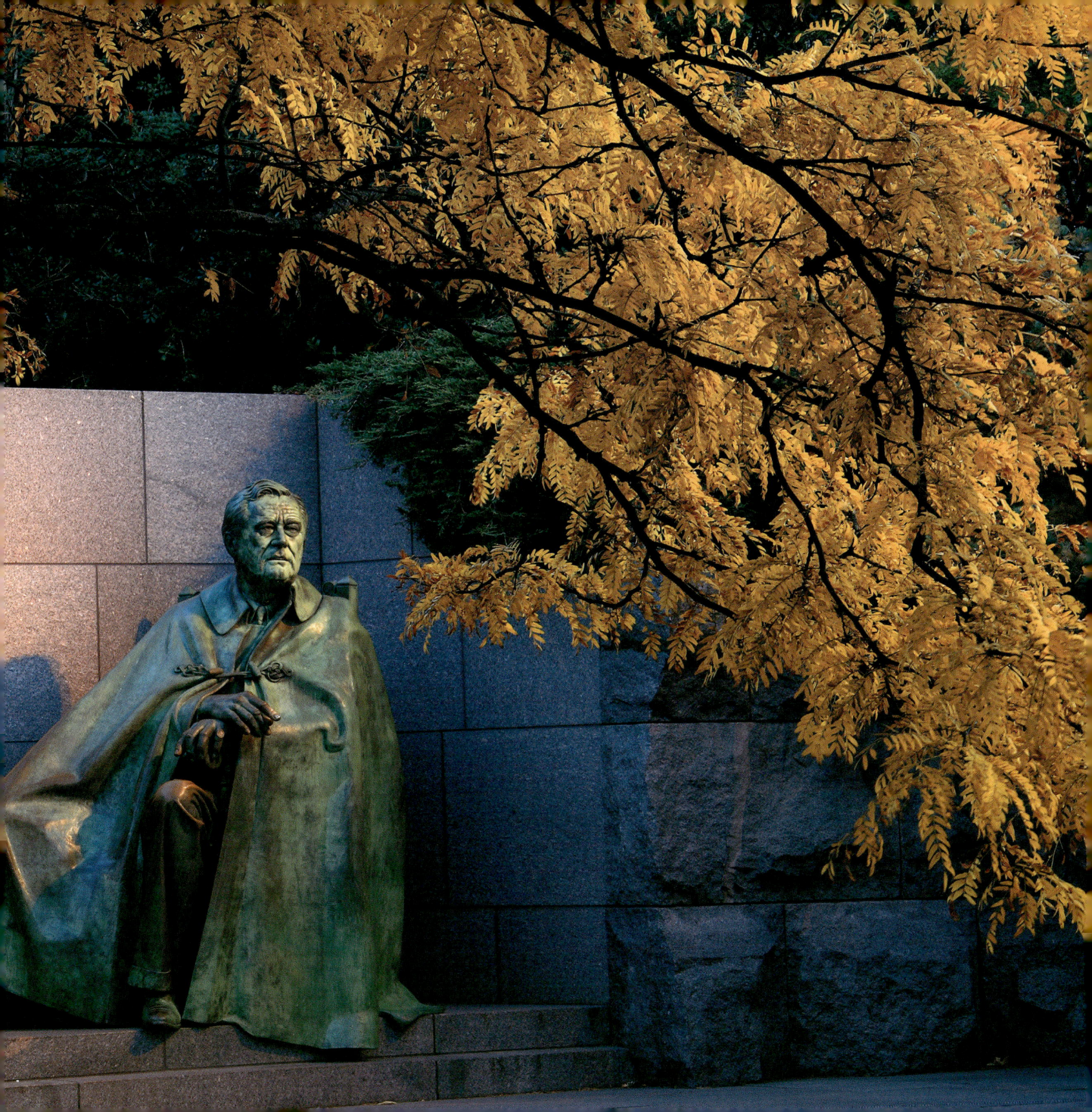

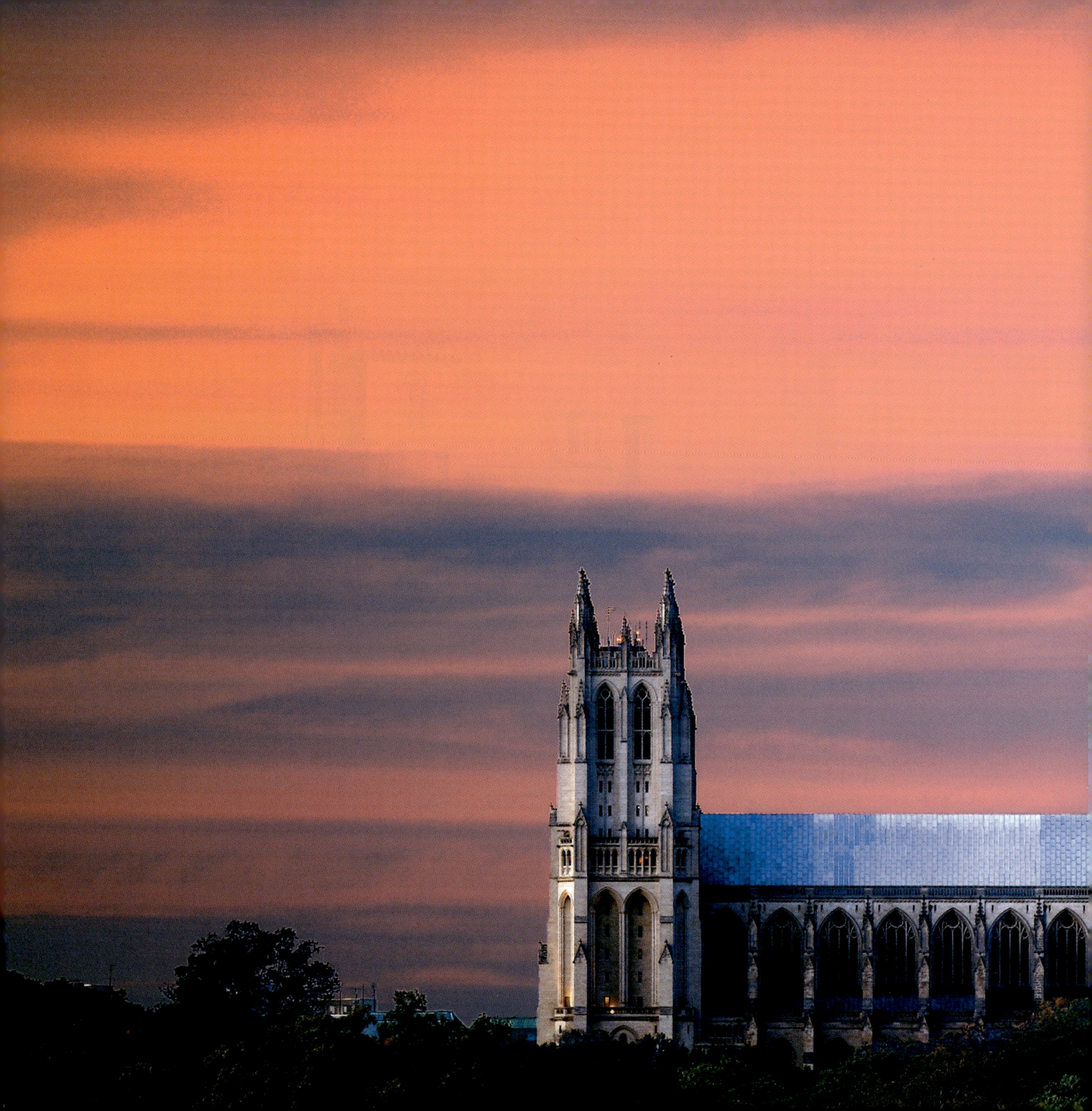

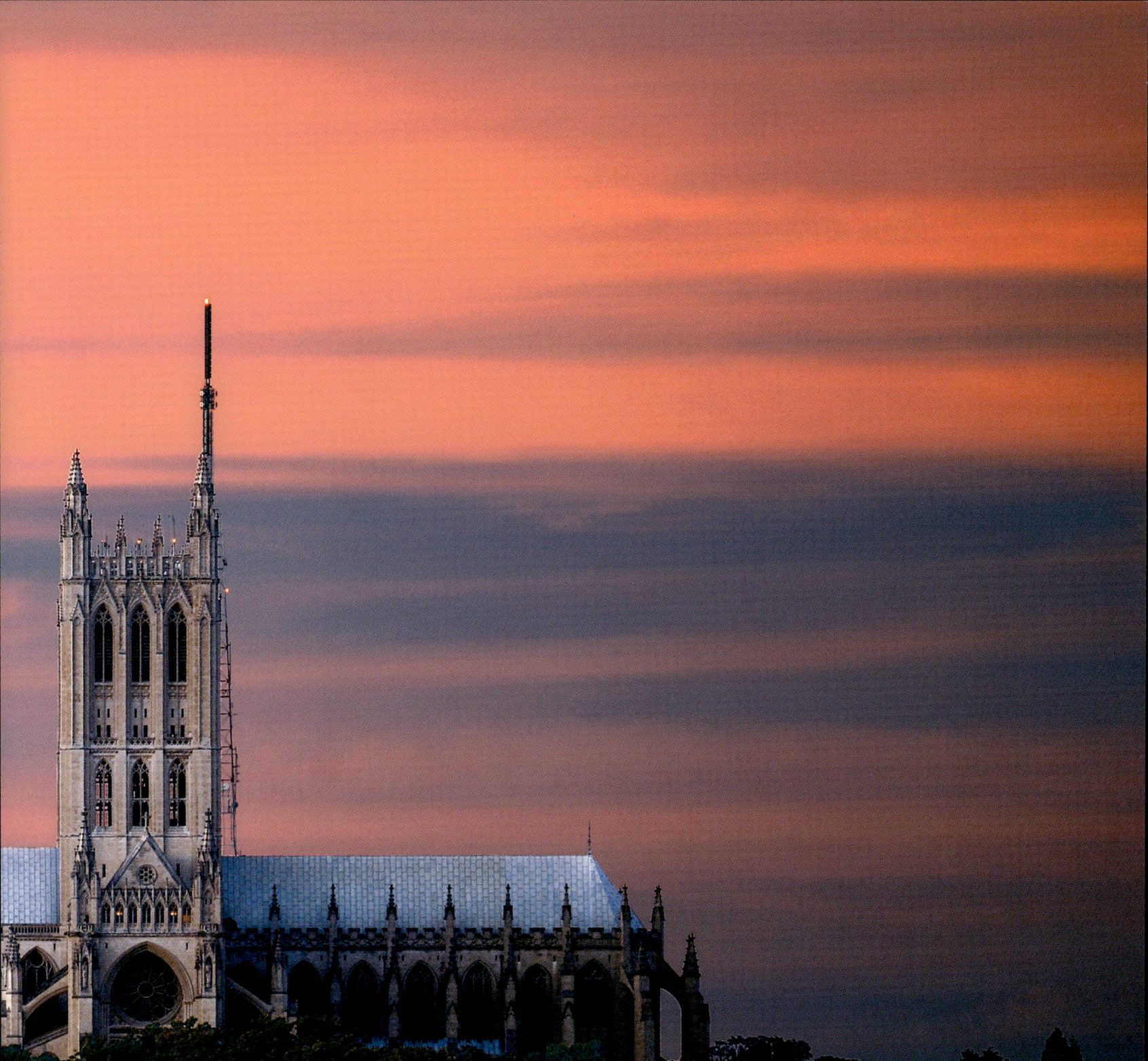

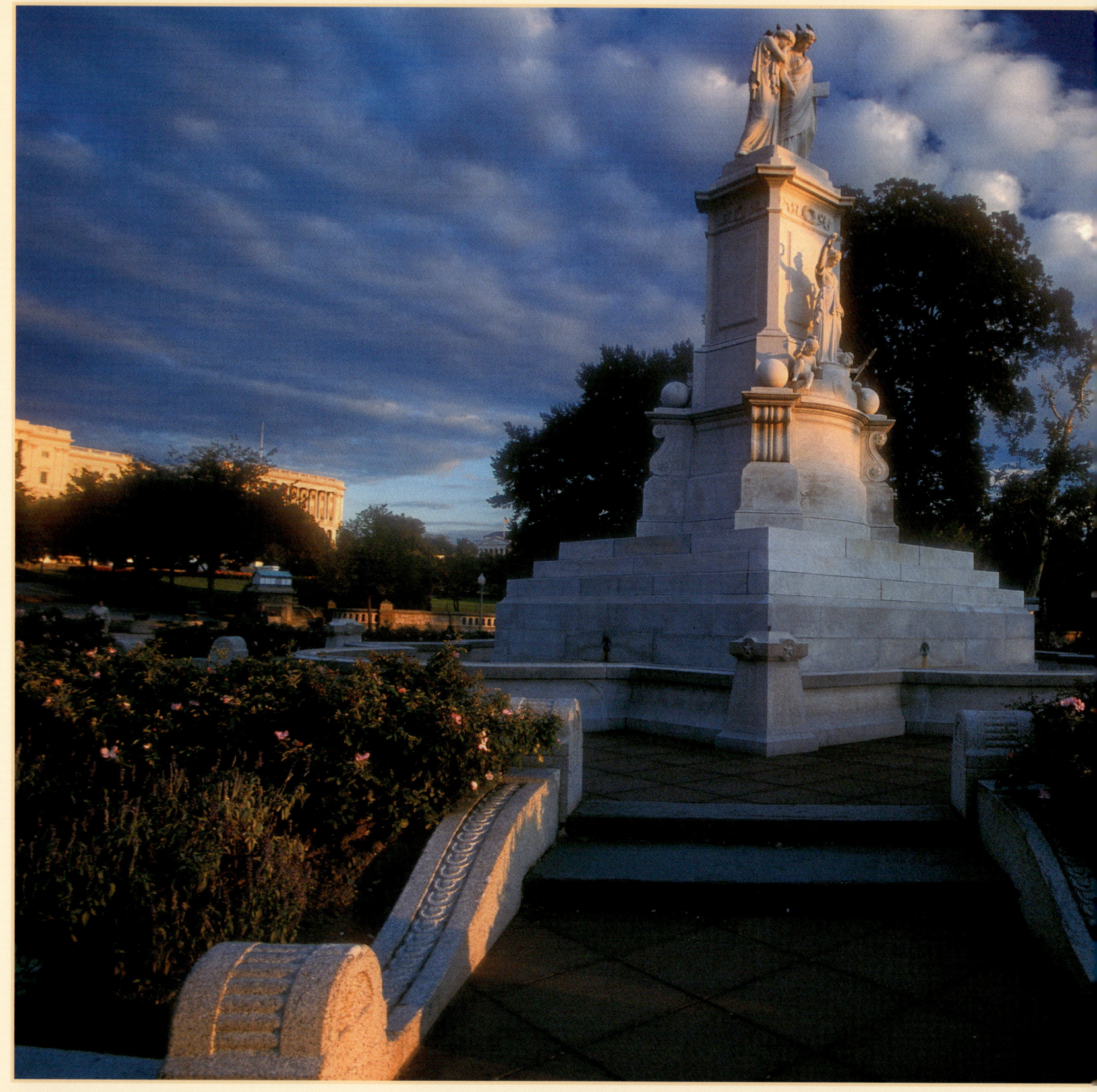

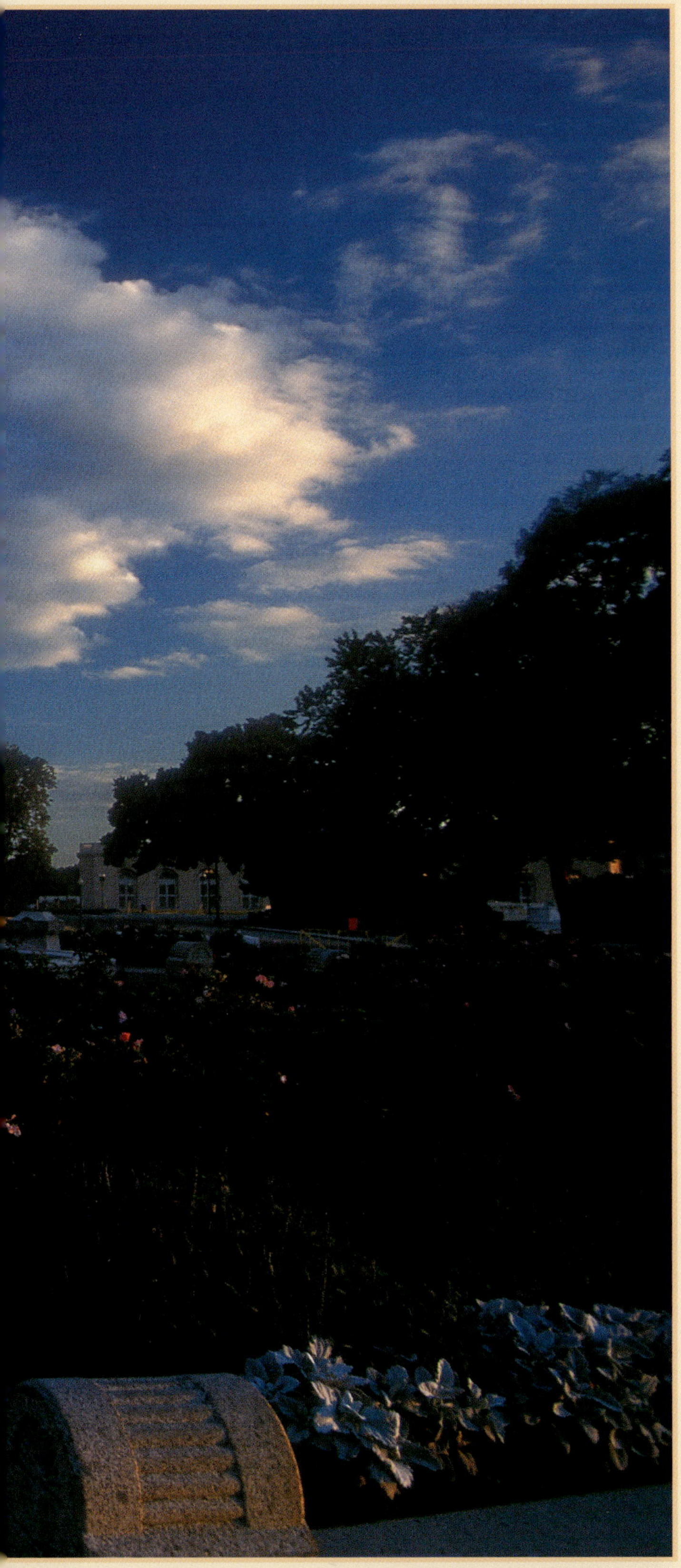

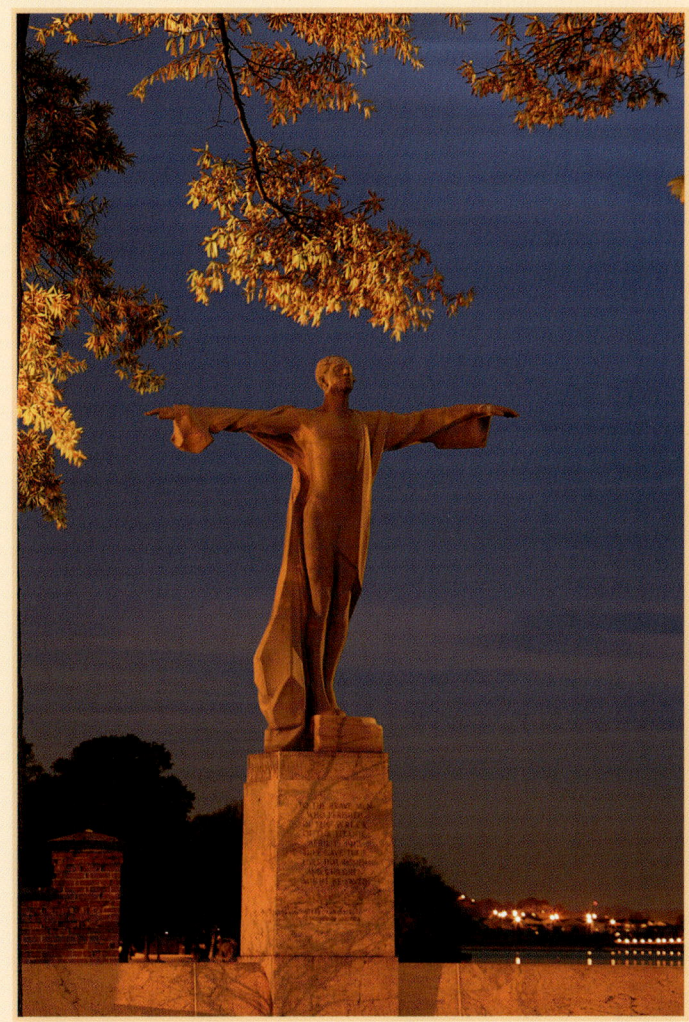

C LOUDS PASS OVER the Peace Monument, standing sentinel in front of the U.S. Capitol.

Above: Memorial to the men of the Titanic in Washington, D.C.'s Southwest Waterfront.

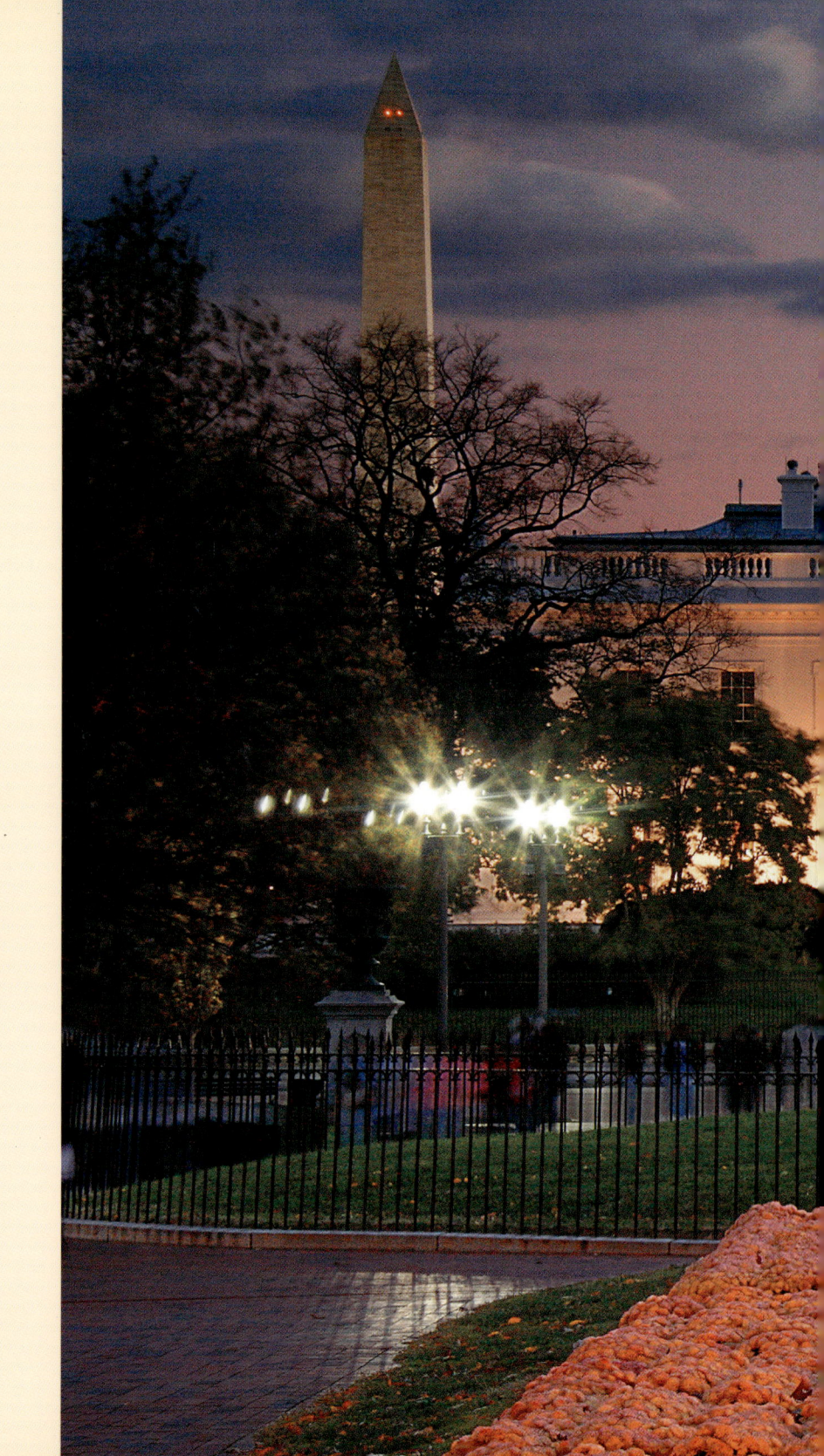

EVENING SETTLES over the White House grounds. The White House, home of the President of the United States, is one of the most famous landmarks worldwide. A statue of Andrew Jackson riding his horse lies in silhouette in the foreground, while the Washington Monument stands like a silent sentinel in the background.

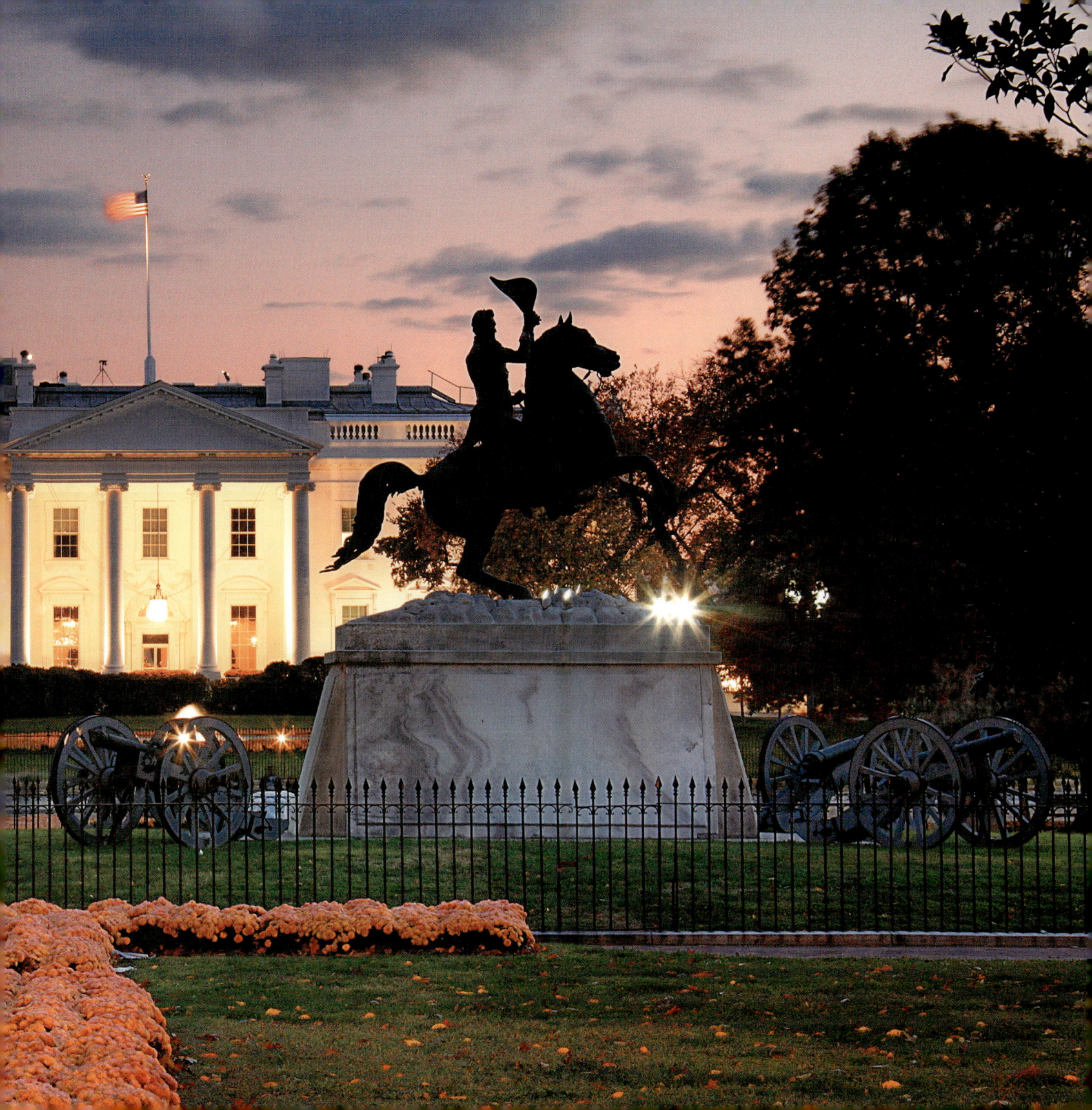

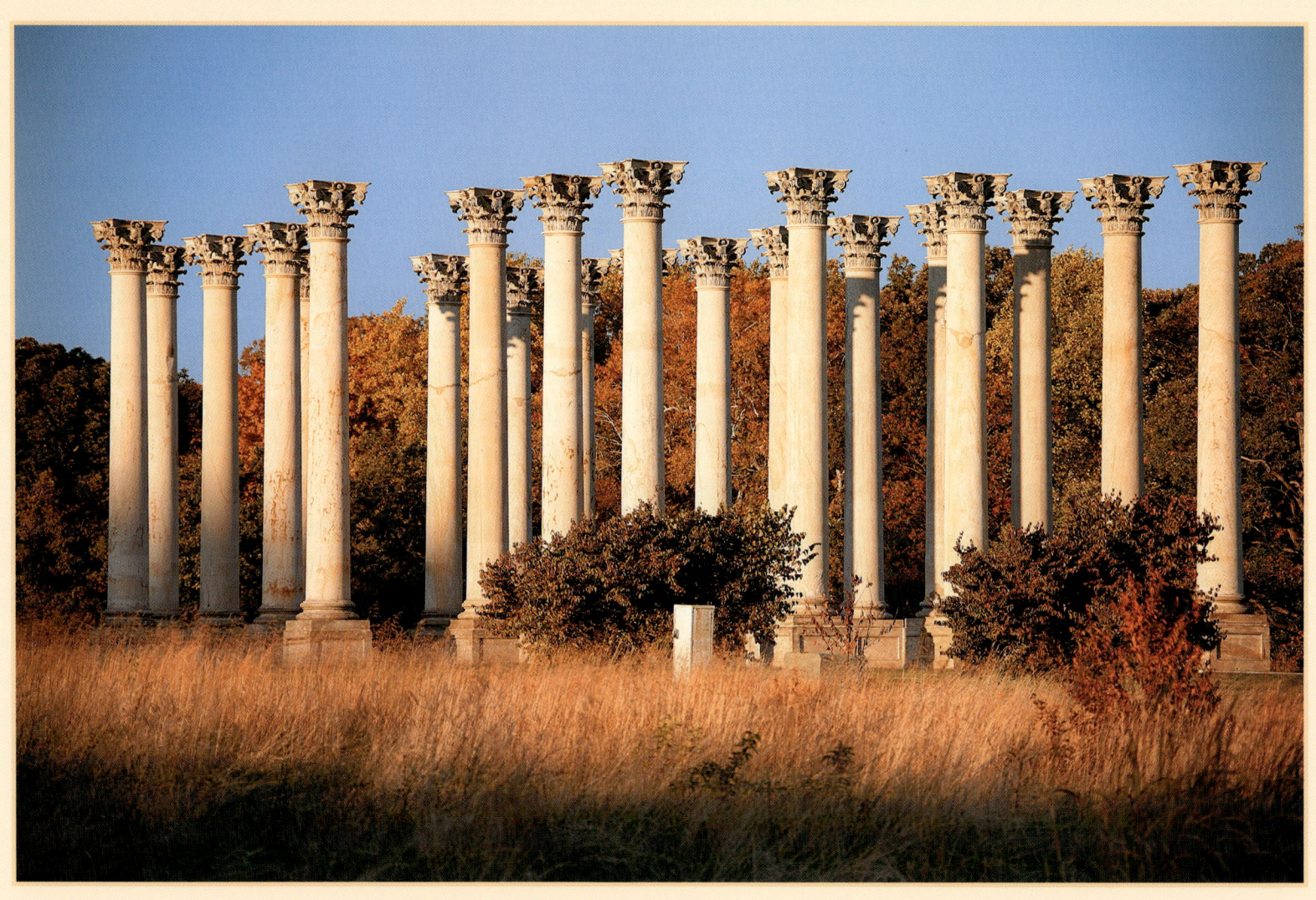

The National Capitol Columns rise above the United States National Arboretum. Originally part of the Capitol Building, these Corinthian-style columns were moved to the Arboretum in 1984.

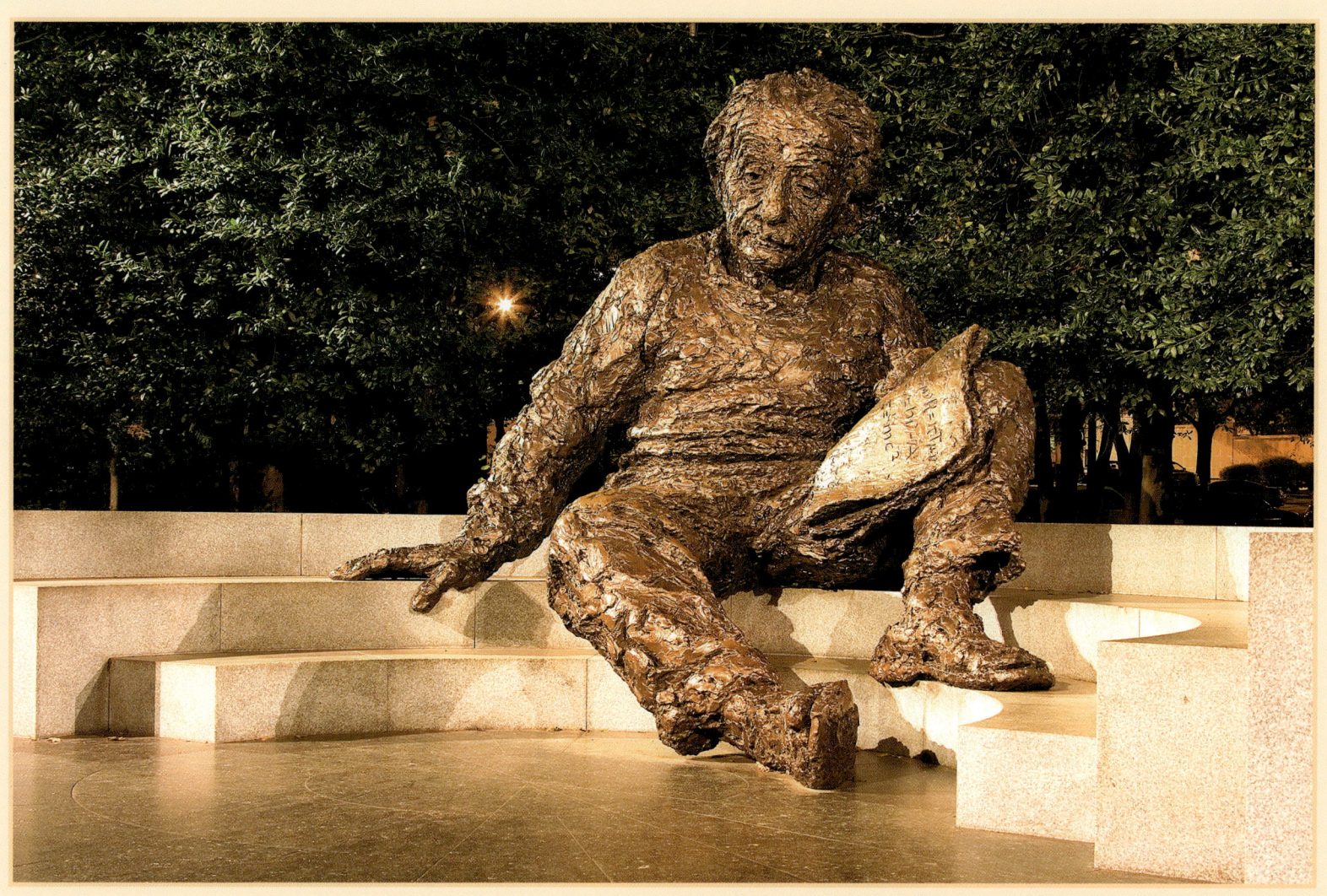

The Albert Einstein Memorial, a fitting tribute to a man who revolutionized several areas of theoretical physics in the 20th Century, is as eccentric as Einstein himself.

Next page: Cheetah cubs playing at the National Zoo's Cheetah Conservation Station.

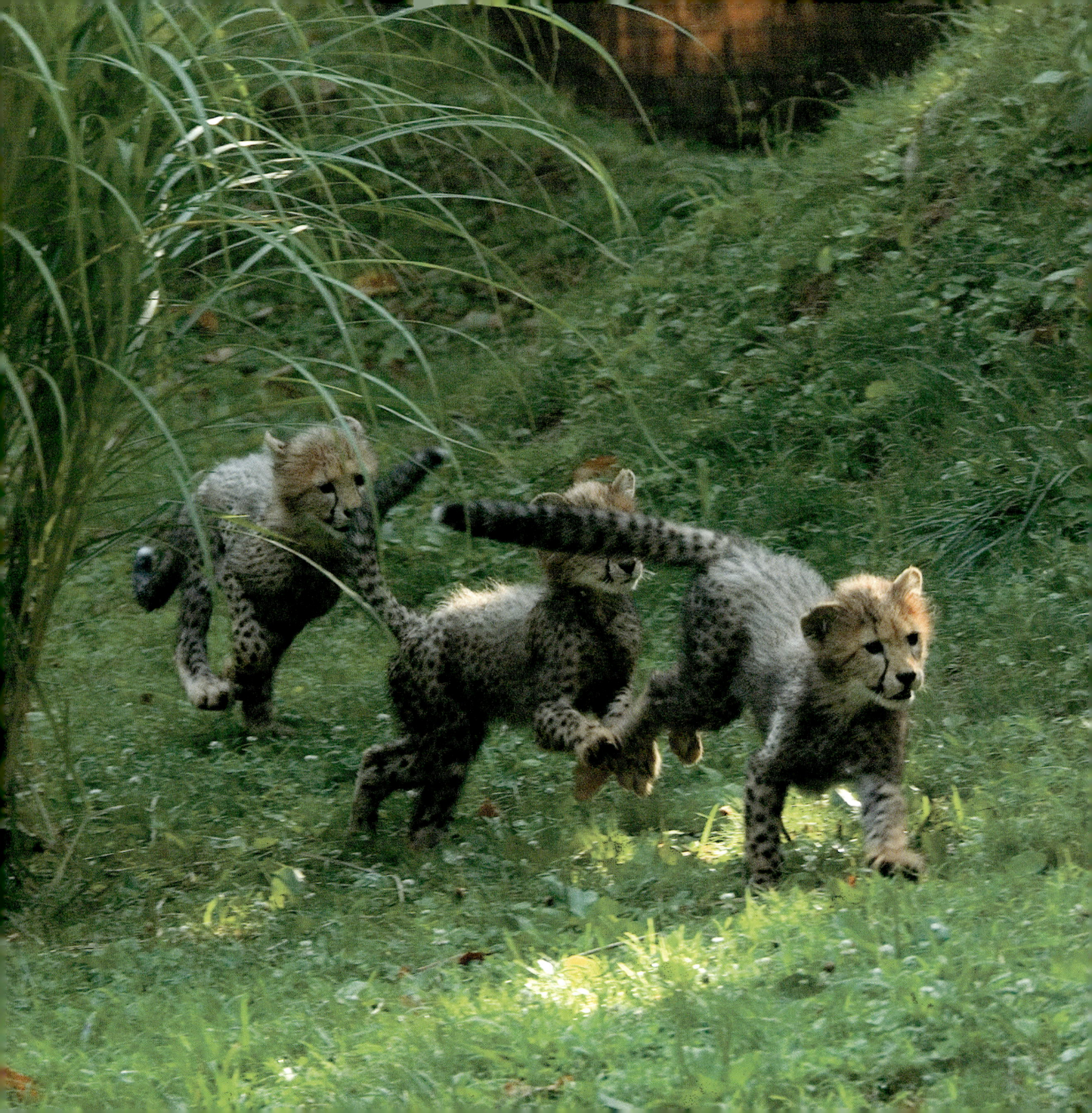

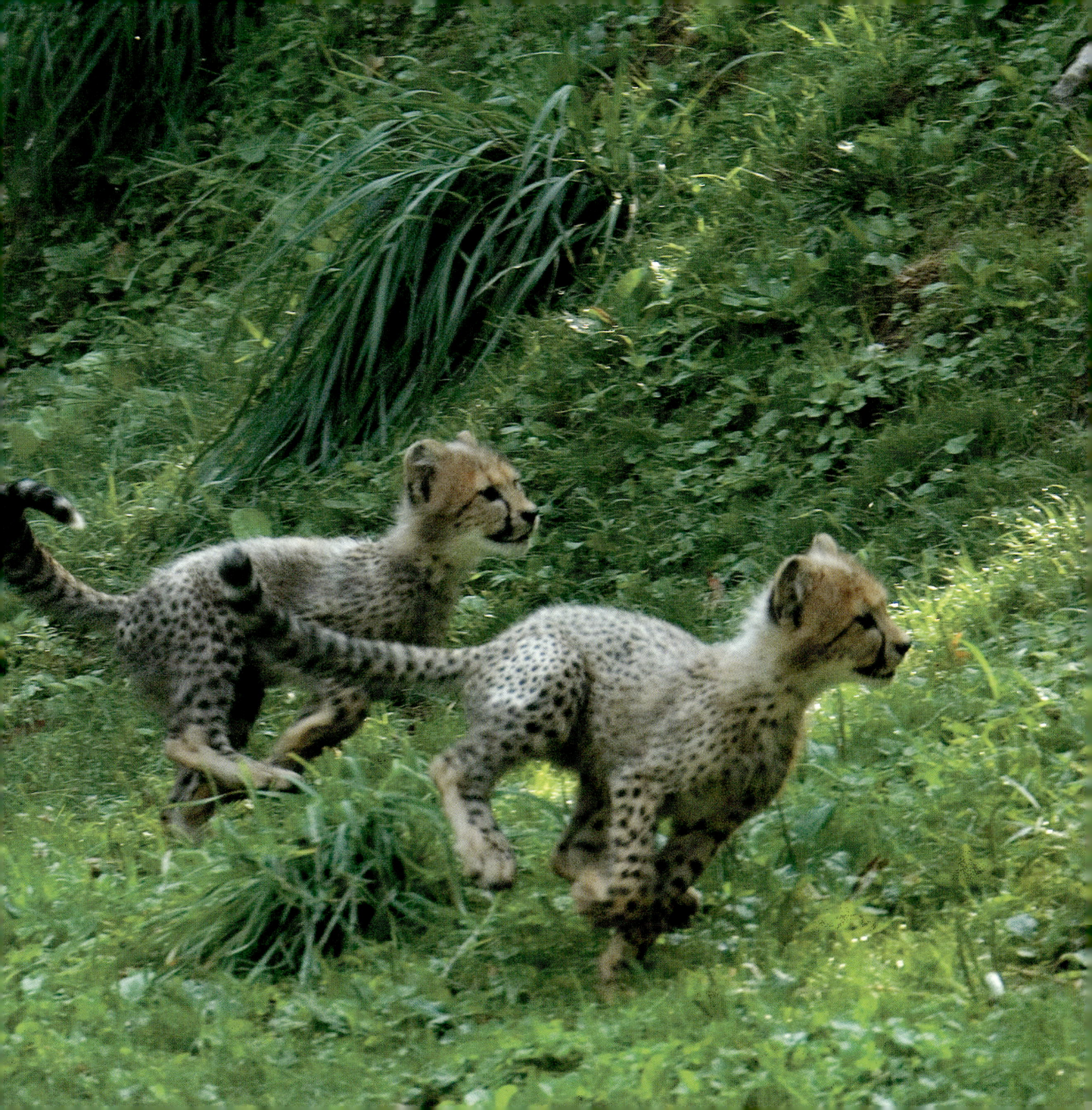

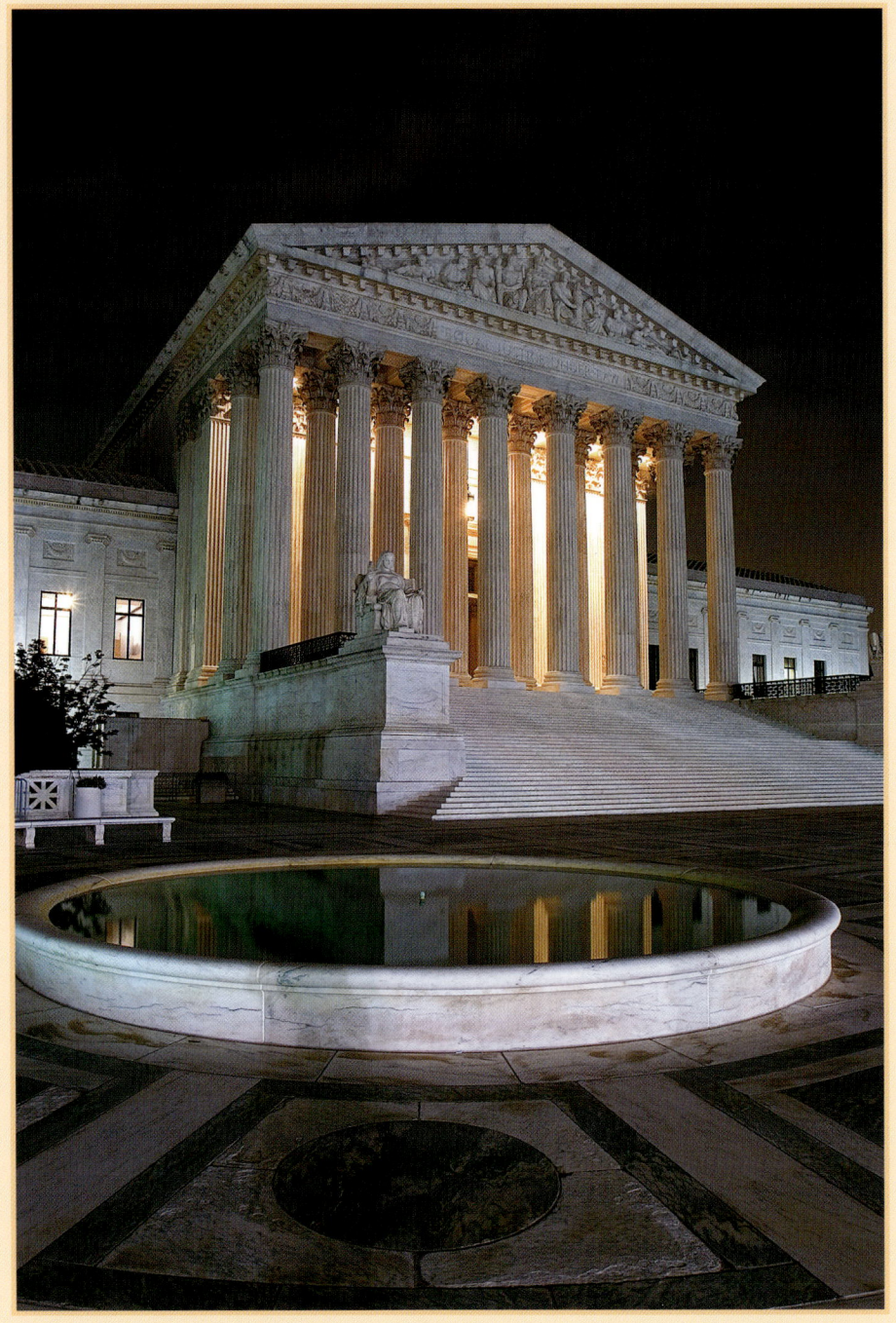

The United States Supreme Court Building at night.

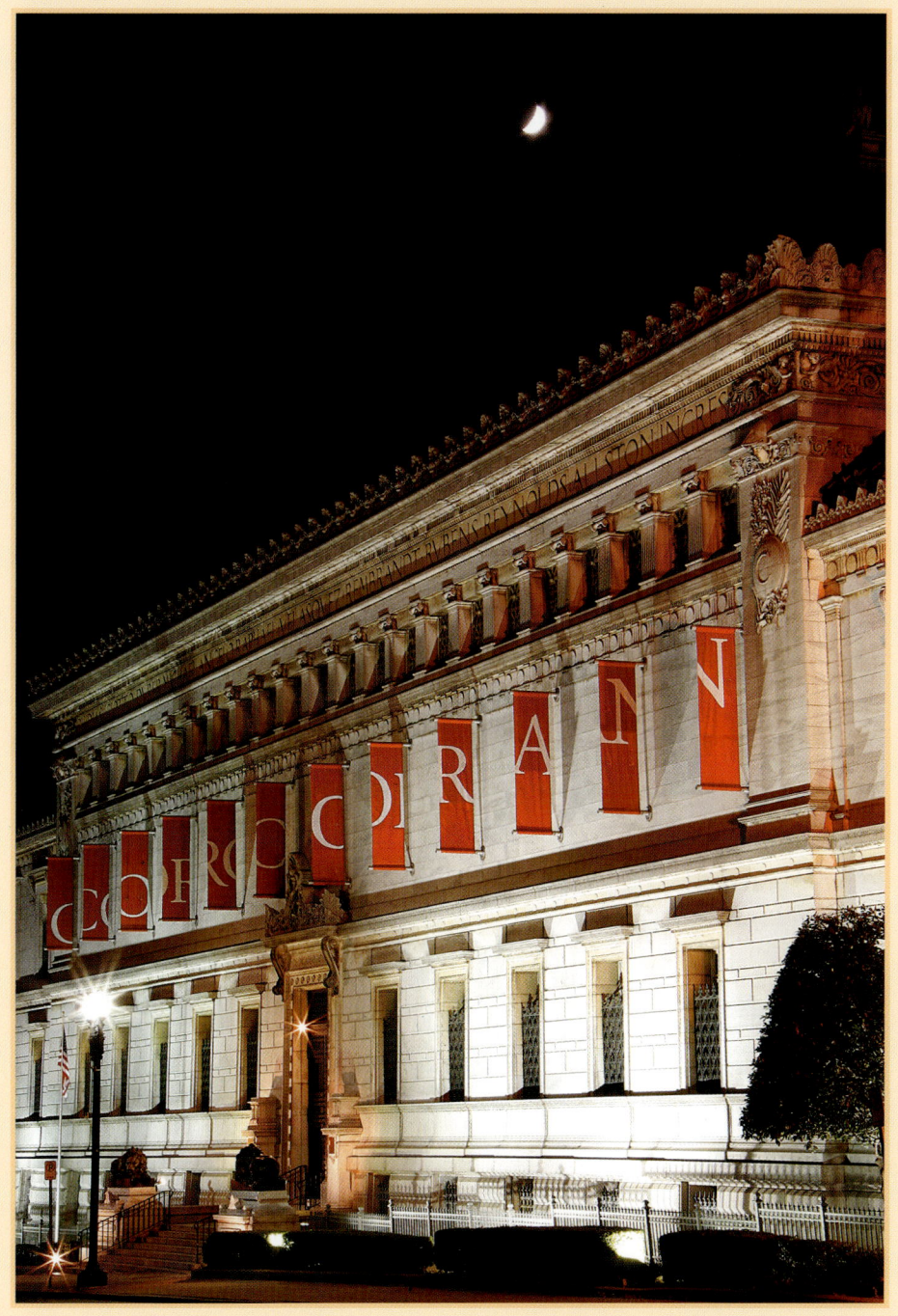

The moon in the night sky over the Corcoran Gallery of Art.

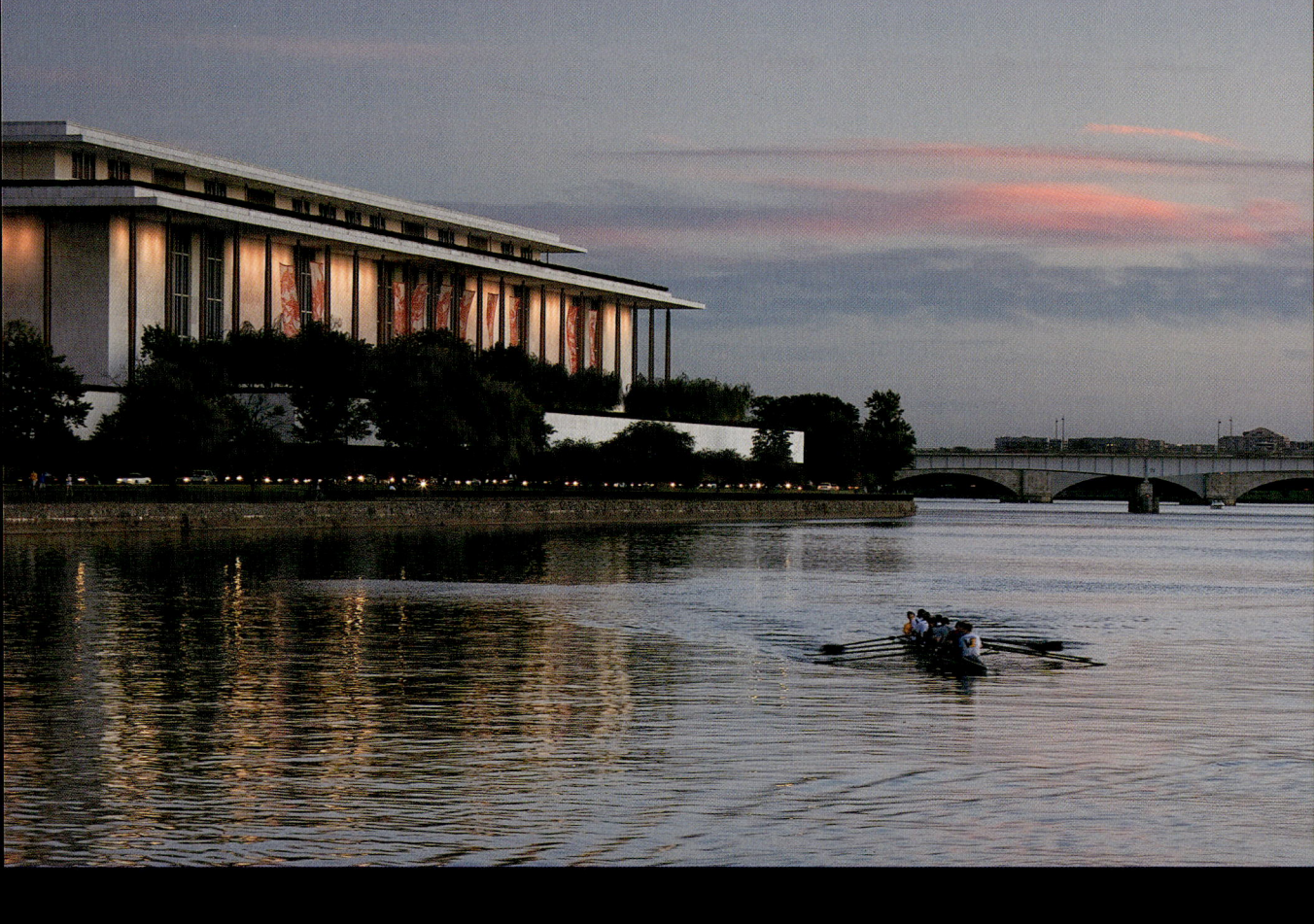

A CREW TEAM paddles in rhythm on the Potomac River below the John F. Kennedy Center For The Performing

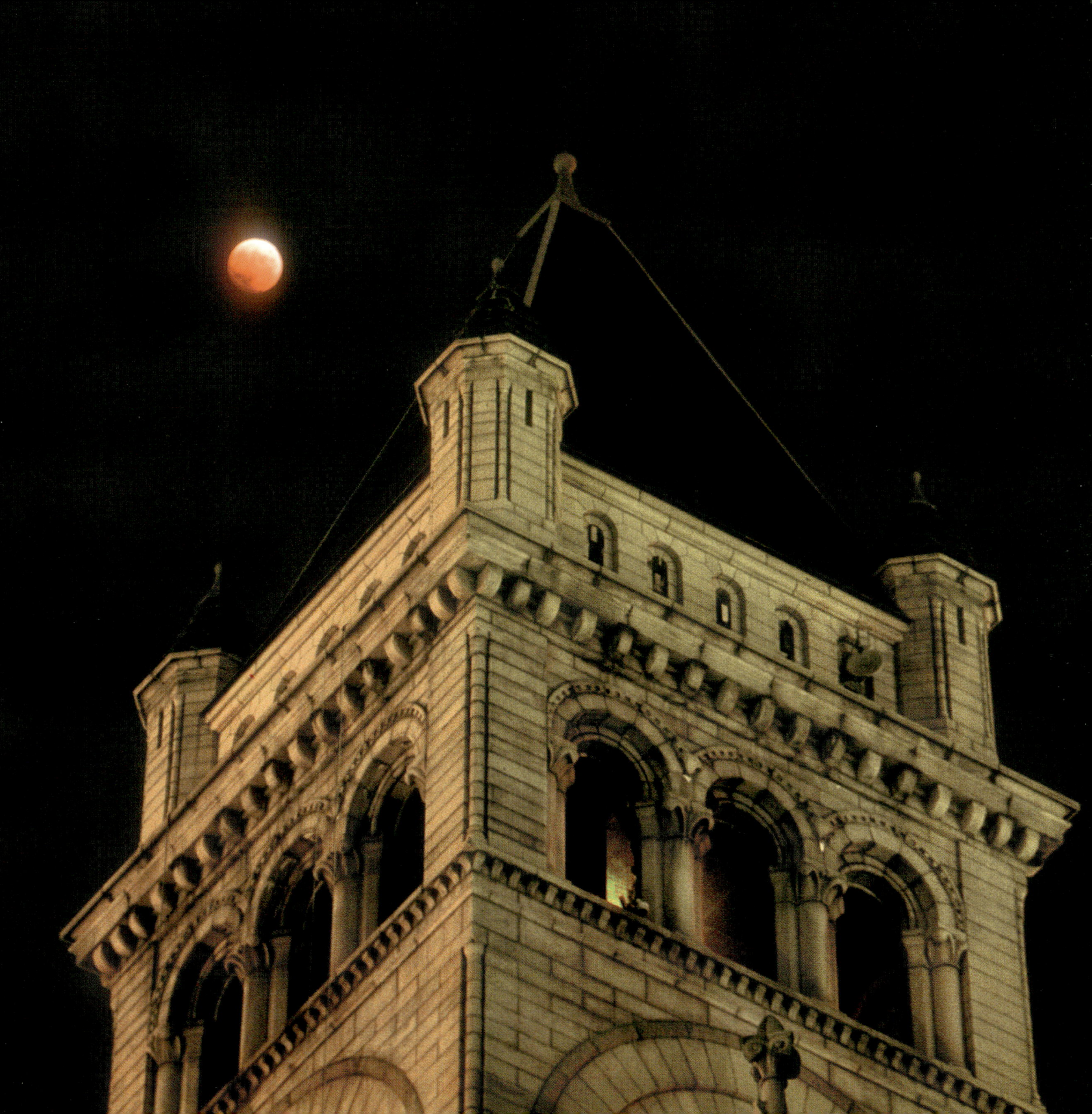

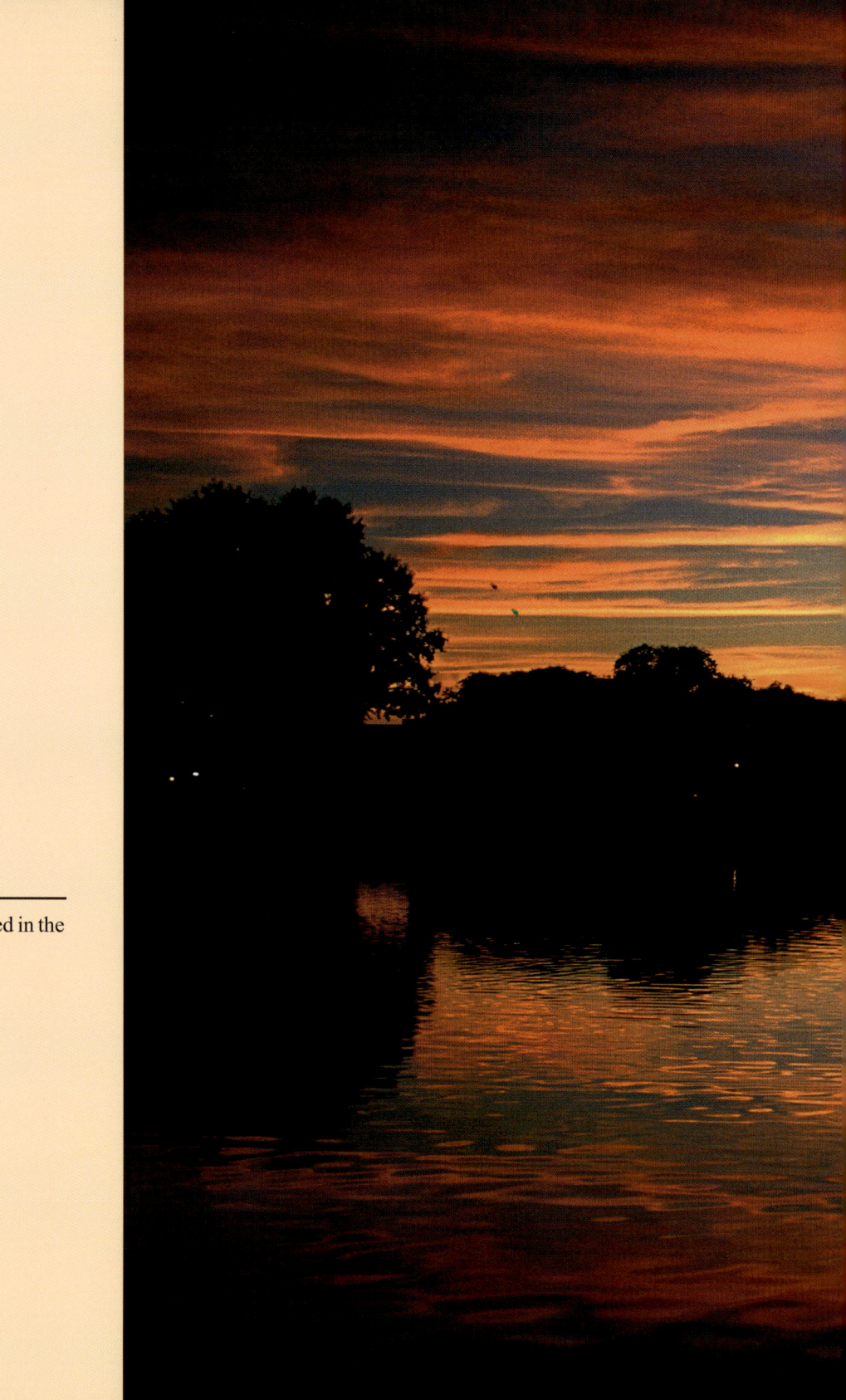

F IERY REDS AND YELLOWS of sunset are reflected in the Capitol Reflecting Pool.

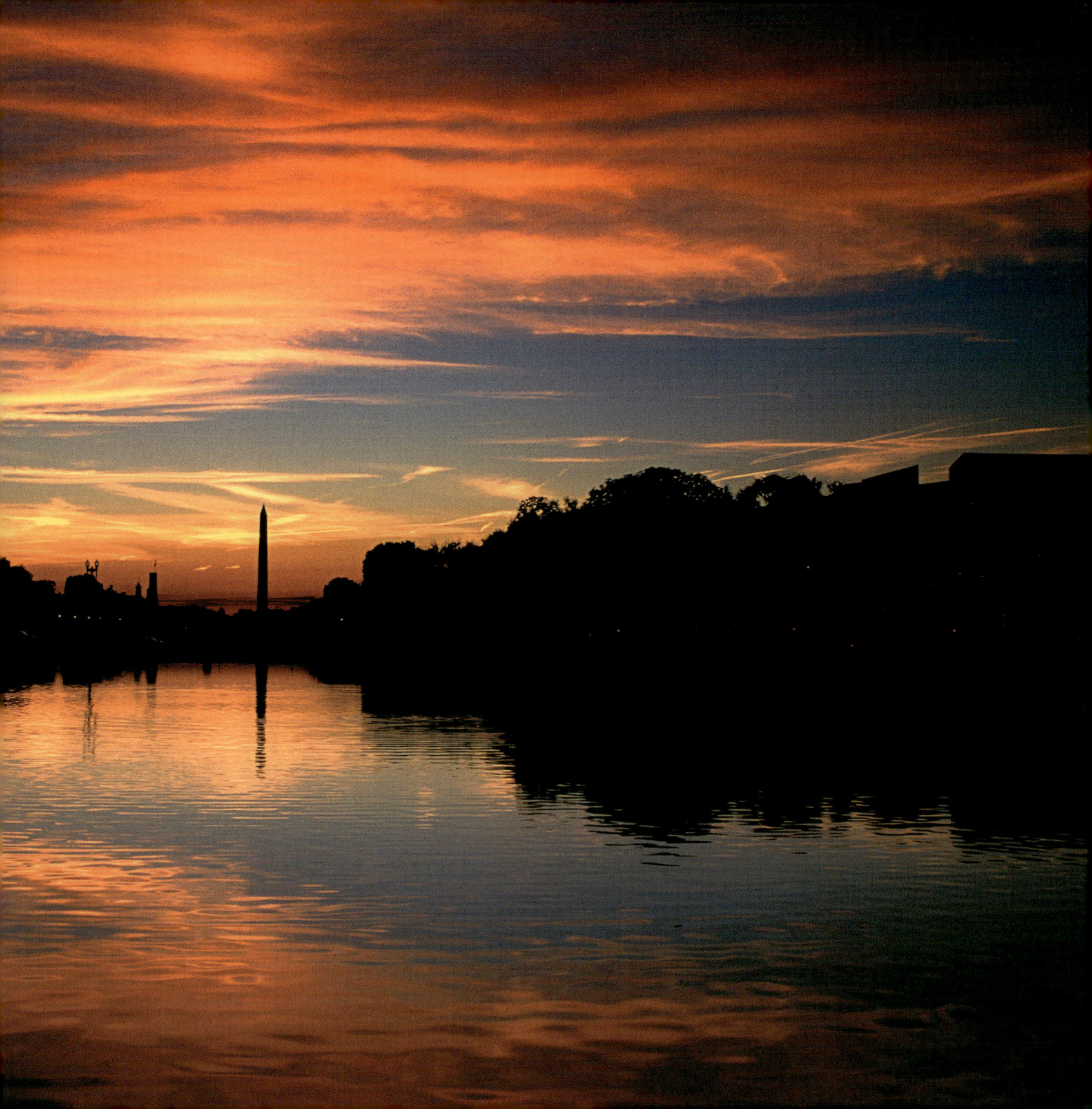

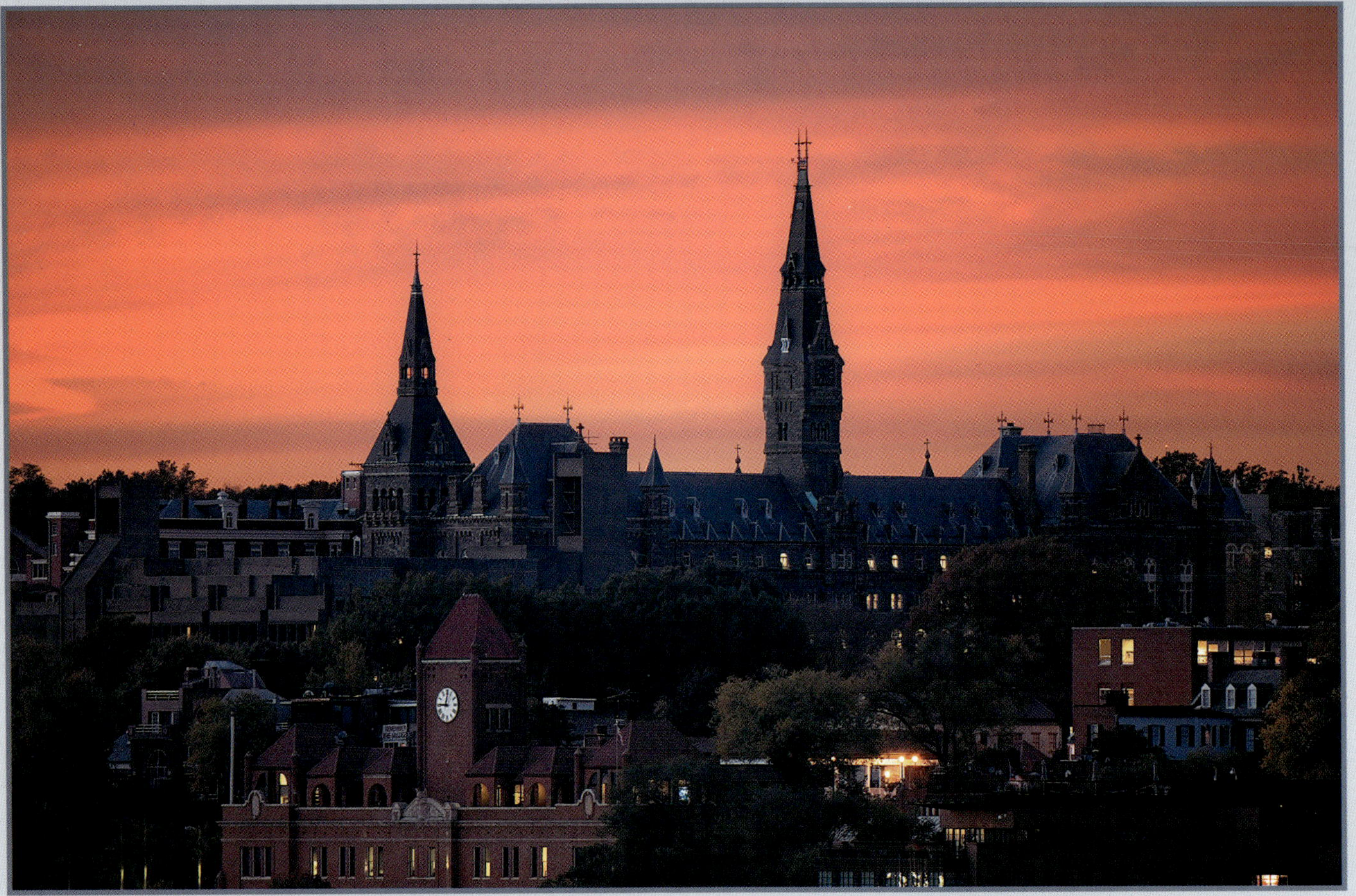

The somber, grey towers of Georgetown University seem austere and forbidding, silhouetted against a flamboyant backdrop of sunset colors splashed across the sky.

About the Photographer: Jean-Louis Monfraix bought his first camera while touring as lead guitarist for the "East Coast Brass" in 1978 and has been capturing his view of life on film ever since. Jean-Louis is also a naturalist and biologist, holding a Master's Degree in Zoology from the University of Florida, and has taught biology as an adjunct professor at the American University in Washington, D.C. and at Santa Fe Community College in Gainesville, Florida. Today, Jean-Louis is one of Washington, D.C's premier photographers. He displays his work at the outdoor markets of the historic Eastern Market on Capitol Hill where he is a successful and well-known vendor. His photographs have appeared in numerous regional publications, and some of his images are part of a permanent exhibition at the Florida State Museum of Natural History. This is his first book.

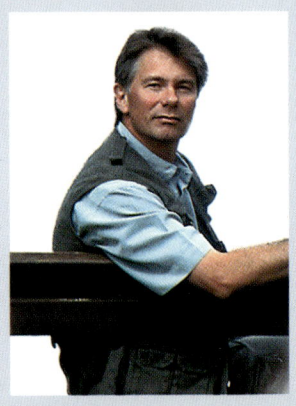

JLMview.com
To see more of Jean-Louis' work, visit his website at www.JLMview.com where you can browse online galleries of photos of Washington, D.C., as well as view other photography by Jean-Louis. You can also get information on how to purchase beautiful, signed, fine art prints of Jean-Louis' photographs.